THE HAPPY PEAR

Recipes for Happiness

Delicious, easy veggie food to be at your best

DAVID & STEPHEN FLYNN

Photography by Alistair Richardson

PENGUIN

IRELAND

TO ALL OF OUR HEALTH
& HAPPINESS ☺

CONTENTS

INTRODUCTION

Greetings and welcome to recipes for health, happiness (and handstands)!

If you are looking at this book you are probably curious about the benefits of plant-based eating. But the book is about so much more than food and nutrition – it's about making you feel good. Eat this way and you'll feel healthier, lose excess weight if you need to, sleep better and be more energetic. Generally you'll feel happier in your skin and be more confident! They are big claims, but these really are the benefits of adopting some of the habits of this book.

Many of you know us from our two previous books, but for those of you who don't, we are Dave and Steve, two plant-powered twins. We started the Happy Pear in 2004 after we had changed from a traditional 'meat and two veg' diet to a whole-food plant-based diet and felt amazing.

Eating more healthily was a gateway to other positive changes. For instance, somehow yoga snuck into our lives. Dave was travelling through Central America in 2001 and kept meeting people who were evangelizing the benefits of yoga. Being an ex-rugby player, he was not convinced. Then a pretty girl lured him into joining a class and he discovered yoga was totally for real men! Since then yoga and movement have been a part of our lives most days and really make us feel better. And exploring plant-based eating and yoga got us more interested in community and nature.

When we started the Happy Pear we had a dream of making the world a healthier, happier place and having lots of fun along the way. Fourteen years later we have three cafés and shops, an online community approaching one million people, a farm, a coffee roastery and a load of wholesome products available across Ireland (and beyond). We never expected to be where we are – or who we are – today!

Just because this is our third book does not mean that the recipes are more complicated. If anything, this is our most user-friendly book yet. We really want to make healthy eating as accessible, practical and budget-friendly as possible. Whether you're cooking for your eight-year-old and her friends, your teenage son, or your dad who's been a meat and spuds man all his life, we reckon you'll be able to flick open any page in this book and get cracking on making a gorgeous, healthy meal that you can have on the table in no time. We have focused a lot on mains in this book – so there is a section called Super Quick Dinners that does what it says on the tin (you'll do most of these recipes in 15 minutes, 20 tops); I Can't Believe It's Not . . . has our versions of popular favourites (kebabs, mac 'n' cheese, sausage rolls . . . steak, even!); and when you have a bit more time, or are cooking for a special occasion, there are gorgeous dinners in Worth the Wait Mains (comfort foods like lasagne and goulash, a scrumptious Wellington and a cracking roast with all the trimmings). Though we say 'worth the wait', most of the recipes in this section are not hugely time-consuming or complicated – we just can't say they're super-quick! As usual we have yummy breakfast and brunch options, and some totally awesome desserts and sweet treats. And because so many people are now into pickling and fermentation, we have a great section to get you going at home – you'll be amazed how easy it is.

The book is called *Recipes for Happiness* and we have taken that very seriously, while having lots of fun with it. The section called Living Happy will walk you through our insights into living a healthier, happier, more balanced life. We are really excited about our two-week health reboot. We have tried to make it as easy as possible for you – it's fast (less than an hour to prepare your food for a week), cheap (apart from store-cupboard basics, food for the week costs less than €25/£22), and requires no homework (we provide shopping lists and a meal prep plan). It's a two-week plant-based adventure, a journey in search of your better self!

Living a healthy lifestyle has become mainstream now and we're inspired to see that so many who might have been suspicious about our 'hippy ways' are now trying, and even embracing, this way of life. However, nutrition is up there with religion and politics in terms of strong feelings and controversy. This book is not about converting you to become a vegetarian or a vegan. We have first-hand experience of the massive benefits of increasing your plant intake and we want to share that with you. But we don't believe that one size fits all. We share our recipes and observations so you can see how this way of eating and living fits into your life – if this simply means starting with some healthier cake or a meat-free Monday, the most important thing is to give it a go!

So please, dive into this book with an open mind and an appetite for trying something new and delicious. We hope that eating more whole plant foods will be the catalyst to much positive change in your life, as it has been in ours!

Dave & Steve

PS We have a huge catalogue of recipe videos on our YouTube channel. While we do not have matching videos for all the recipes in this book there are quite a few. Each recipe chapter has a list of the featured recipes at the start - look for this icon ▶ in the listing to see which ones have an online video. You can find the videos via thehappypear.ie – click on the 'recipes' tab and search. Or go straight to our YouTube channel (just search 'The Happy Pear' to locate it). Our demos don't match the recipes word for word but will show you the method and how things are supposed to turn out.

PART I
EATING HAPPY

CUPBOARD ESSENTIALS & KITCHEN KIT

CUPBOARD ESSENTIALS

STARCH

Being Irish, we've stayed true to our roots and embraced the humble oat! Whether it be to bump up a veggie burger, part of a breakfast smoothie or in its most wholesome form – as porridge – we can't get enough of the stuff. We love nothing more than kicking the day off with a big bowl of porridge made with oat milk and topped with our favourites – figs, coconut yoghurt, granola, maybe some fruit compote . . . Starting the day off with this slow-releasing energy source keeps us on form for the rest of the day and we couldn't rate it highly enough.

We'll always have some form of wholegrain cracker in our cupboards. We go for Ryvita, as it's cheap and keeps for ages. These are an easy base for our much-loved on-the-go open sandwiches!

Wholemeal couscous takes 5 minutes to cook and you can include whatever spices/salt/pepper you like. Literally all you need to do is cover the couscous up to just above the surface with boiling water, cover with a lid, leave for 5 minutes and it's done.

Brown rice. Short-grain is that bit nuttier and more flavoursome than long-grain basmati.

Quinoa is another staple that you just can't go wrong with. Can also be used in salads if the weather is hot and you want to keep things light.

Wholemeal pasta. Our preference is fusilli. If you're gluten-free, brown rice pasta is a good option.

NUTS, BEANS AND PULSES

The age-old question: 'How do people on a plant-based diet get their protein?' Well, here's a list of great sources of plant-based protein.

Nuts. Our favourites are walnuts, almonds and pecans.

Almond butter — but any nut butter does the job.

Light tahini butter (the dark tahini butter is a bit more earthy and slightly less palatable).

Red lentils. We mostly use these for dahls, but they're also great for soups when you have leftover veg. Just put the veg, lentils and some spices to liven things up in a pot, together with water or vegetable stock, bring to the boil, simmer for about 15 minutes and wham bam, you've got yourself a healthy, super-nutritious soup/dinner!

Canned beans are really handy to have in the cupboard. Chickpeas, butter beans, black beans and kidney beans work really well in curries and stews to bump up the nutritional profile and make things go a little further on the cheap. You can also blend these to form the base of a gorgeous, nourishing hummus or your plant-based spread of choice!

CONDIMENTS

Tamari. This is just soy sauce that has been aged for longer and is gluten-free. Dave loves the softer, sweeter umami flavour that it gives to food.

Liquid sweetener. We go for maple syrup, but it can be expensive, so this depends on whatever your budget can allow.

Nutritional yeast, or 'nooch' (as it's often referred to in North America). This is a great one for anyone following a dairy-free/plant-based/vegan lifestyle, as it adds a 'cheesy' flavour to food and is also packed with vitamin B12.

SAUCES

Tinned tomatoes and tomato purée (or tomato concentrate). Vital for any tomato-based sauce.

Coconut milk. Full-fat is typically 20% fat content, while low-fat is generally about 10%. Scoop the solid fat off the top of the liquid and whip it to make a great alternative to dairy cream (it goes lovely with raspberry jam!).

Vegetable stock. Great for soups – just have a look at the ingredients when you're buying it and try to get one that's lower in salt.

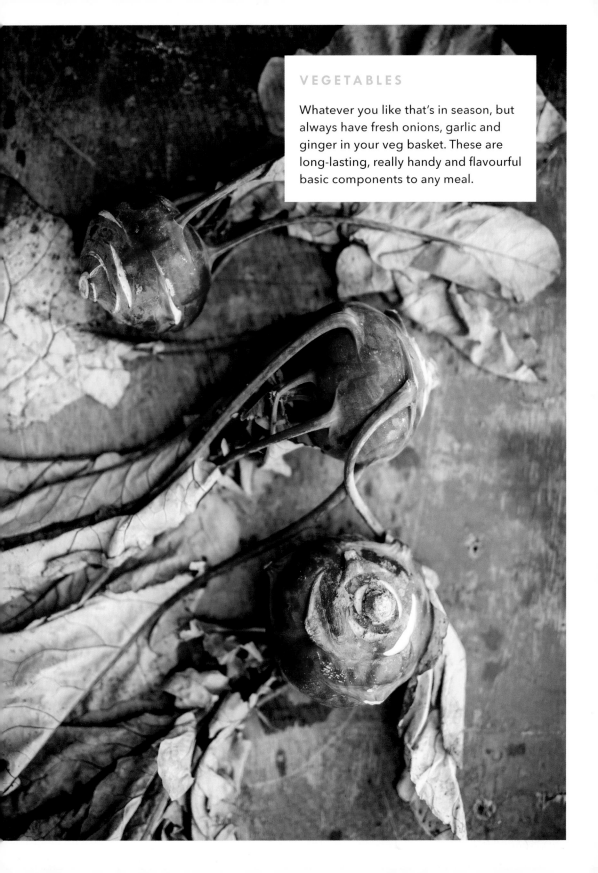

VEGETABLES

Whatever you like that's in season, but always have fresh onions, garlic and ginger in your veg basket. These are long-lasting, really handy and flavourful basic components to any meal.

SPICES

Ground cumin. Use in everything.

Smoked paprika. Adds a lovely smoky meaty flavour and works great in chilli. A little goes a long way, so use lightly!

Ground coriander. Not for everyone, but we're big fans!

Chilli flakes. These are great for anyone who can handle a bit of heat. They add a lovely texture and colour to whatever dish you decide to sprinkle them in.

Medium curry powder. A brilliant way to liven up a dish! Mix with a few tablespoons of coconut milk and you've got yourself the easiest sauce going.

OTHER

Non-dairy milks. You can get these in every health food store, and we're delighted that they are now more readily available in supermarkets too. We recommend going for the unsweetened versions, to keep your sugar levels even.

Oils. We try to limit our use of oils (see page 271 for our two cents on oil). That aside, we have olive, sunflower and rapeseed oils in our kitchens. Our friend Keith lives near us in Wicklow and grows and presses his own rapeseed (Wicklow Rapeseed), so this tends to be our default option. However, rapeseed has a distinct taste. Sunflower is typically more neutral-tasting, while olive oil can often be . . . grassy or olive-tasting! Depending on your needs, each has its own purpose.

KITCHEN KIT

Here are a few bits and bobs that we use time and time again. We have accumulated these over time, so pick and choose what you think you will use and build up your own kit.

A decent food processor. We use this a lot for the bases of desserts and for whizzing up many of our snacks.

A stick blender. Great for blending soups. These are usually inexpensive and are well worth having. You can use a food processor, of course, but it can be a lot messier.

A high-speed blender. A regular blender will do fine for most things, but if you want to grind flax seeds, turn quinoa or oat flakes into flour, or want super-smooth smoothies, a regular blender usually won't do this.

A sharp chopping knife. We are often asked what type of knife we would recommend, and our answer is always a sharp one. A blunt knife is the most dangerous knife in the kitchen. A sharp chef's knife will do the job for most things. We do use a serrated knife too (e.g. a bread knife), for tomatoes, aubergines and other thick-skinned veg.

A decent non-stick frying pan. Essential if you make pancakes. If your pan is not non-stick, you will need to use more oil and things will stick so much more.

Decent medium and large pots/ saucepans. Again, non-stick versions will make life easier. For the last couple of years we have been using Circulon products, which are great. Our preference is for heavy-based, wide-bottomed, shallower pots/pans rather than taller ones.

Finally, **oven temperatures** . . . all electric oven temperatures in the recipes are for a conventional oven. If you use a fan oven, simply reduce the temperature given by 20°C/35°F.

PUMPKIN SPICED LATTE PANCAKES / FRENCH TOAST ▶ / HEALTHY WAFFLES ▶ / BREAKFAST BURRITO ▶ /

FIVE-MINUTE ONE-PAN GRANOLA ▶ / MEL'S PORRIDGE FOR POWER / ACAI BOWL ▶ /

GREEN POWER SMOOTHIE / SODA BREAD ▶ / GLUTEN-FREE BREAD / OYSTER MUSHROOMS WITH GARLIC,

TOMATOES & WILTED SPINACH

BREKKIE 'N' BRUNCH

PUMPKIN SPICED LATTE PANCAKES

The title says it all. These pancakes make such a tasty breakfast treat, any time of the year. In Ireland tinned pumpkin is not readily available, so we recommend you bake your own pumpkin/butternut squash/sweet potato at 200°C/400°F/Gas Mark 6 for about 30 minutes, scoop out the flesh, and use that.

20 MINS

175g buckwheat flour/
other flour of choice

½ teaspoon sea salt

1 teaspoon baking powder

3 tablespoons pumpkin
purée

1 tablespoon vanilla extract

2 tablespoons maple syrup/
other liquid sweetener

1 teaspoon ground
cinnamon

1 teaspoon ground ginger

½ teaspoon ground
cardamom

½ teaspoon ground allspice

50g cashew nuts

300ml rice milk

1 tablespoon finely ground
coffee (optional but
recommended)

oil, for cooking the pancakes

1. Put all your ingredients, apart from the oil, into a blender and blend until smooth.

2. Place a non-stick frying pan on a high heat. Lightly drizzle some oil into the pan to prevent the mixture from sticking. Once the oil heats up, reduce the heat to medium.

3. Pour enough batter into the pan to lightly cover the surface (about 5 tablespoons for a large pancake and 2–3 for mini ones). Move the pan around to spread the batter out nice and evenly.

4. Once bubbles start to form around the edges and in the middle, and the top starts to dry out, it's time to flip your pancake over and cook on the other side. Once browned on both sides, it's done.

5. Repeat the process until all your pancakes are cooked. Now plate them up and devour.

SOME SERVING IDEAS

Top with maple syrup, banana, fresh berries, almond butter, coconut yoghurt, fresh mango, apricots, passion fruit, cacao nibs, bee pollen, goji berries . . . the list goes on!

FRENCH TOAST

This vegan French toast is a perfect mix of sweet and savoury that will have you dancing round the kitchen on a Sunday morning! Perfect for a weekend brunch or for a special celebratory brekkie. Here we make it with caramelized bananas, which takes it to the next level. Also goes great served with fresh berries, maple syrup and toasted nuts.

15–20 MINS

2 tablespoons olive oil

200ml almond or rice milk

2 tablespoons almond butter

2 tablespoons maple syrup

a pinch of sea salt

1 teaspoon ground cinnamon

½ teaspoon vanilla extract

1 tablespoon ground flax seeds

6–8 slices of white or sourdough bread (stale bread is fine)

1 teaspoon oil

4 bananas

1. Put all the ingredients except the bread, oil and bananas into a blender and whiz together until smooth. Pour into a wide bowl with a flat bottom and soak the bread in this mixture, moving it around and turning, making sure that the bread really absorbs the liquid.

2. Put a non-stick pan on a high heat, add the oil and spread it round the pan. Once hot, reduce the heat to medium-high and add a couple of slices of the soaked bread. Fry for a few minutes on each side, until the bread starts to turn golden on the outside. Once both sides are crispy, remove from the pan. Repeat till all your French toast is done.

3. Prepare your caramelized bananas while the French toast is cooking. Peel the bananas and cut them in half lengthways, then in half the other way, giving you four pieces from each banana. Put a dry pan on a high heat, then add the bananas and dry-fry for a couple of minutes on each side, until they start to char and smell amazing. Serve on top of your French toast, with a drizzle of maple syrup, some berries/other fresh fruit or whatever you fancy.

HEALTHY WAFFLES

This is a great recipe that works perfectly for pancakes too. Dave uses this recipe most weekends to make either pancakes or waffles for his daughters – the same batter works great for both. To make waffles, you will need a waffle iron or waffle maker, but don't let that put you off – we got ours for €20 online and it's a great toy! We like to serve our waffles/pancakes with coconut yoghurt, homemade chocolate spread and berries, with a drizzle of maple syrup – just delish!

20 MINS

250g buckwheat flour/ other flour of choice

2 teaspoons baking powder (1½ teaspoons if using white flour)

1 teaspoon sea salt

3 tablespoons maple syrup

½ a banana or 2 tablespoons ground flax seeds

3 tablespoons almond butter

400ml rice milk

1 teaspoon vanilla extract

1. First step, turn on the waffle iron.

2. To make the batter, whiz all the ingredients together in a blender until smooth.

3. Once the waffle iron is hot, spray it with vegetable oil to prevent the waffles from sticking. Pour in the batter, ensuring that you have added enough to cover the full iron, and leaving a bit of room for the waffles to rise slightly.

4. Cook in the waffle iron until they turn nice and brown. Remove and add toppings of your choice (see intro, and see the photo for other serving ideas).

BREAKFAST BURRITOS

This makes a super-tasty Mexican-style weekend breakfast or brunch. It's full of flavour, with great colours and textures that will satisfy all the family.

10–15 MINS

For the guacamole

2 ripe avocados

juice of 1 lime

½ teaspoon sea salt

a pinch of freshly ground
     black pepper

10 cherry tomatoes

1 teaspoon ground cumin

½ teaspoon chilli flakes

a small bunch of fresh
     coriander

**For the mushrooms with
     spinach**

2 cloves of garlic

150g oyster mushrooms, or
     other mushrooms

1–2 tablespoons oil

3 tablespoons tamari/soy
     sauce

a good handful of fresh
     baby spinach

To assemble

2 x 400g tins of baked beans

4 wholemeal tortilla wraps

1. Start by making the guacamole. Peel and de-stone the avocados and chop the flesh into small pieces. Put into a bowl with the lime juice, salt and black pepper. Chop the cherry tomatoes in half and add, along with the cumin and chilli flakes. Mash with a fork until the avocado breaks up and comes together. Finely chop the coriander (including the stalks) and add. Mix, taste and adjust the seasoning if you think it needs it.

2. Peel and finely chop the garlic and roughly chop the mushrooms. Put the oil into a medium pan on a high heat and leave to heat up. Add the garlic and mushrooms and cook for 1 minute, stirring regularly. Add the tamari and cook for a further 2 minutes. Add the spinach and cook for a further minute, until it wilts right down. Remove from the heat.

3. Put the baked beans into a pan and heat up on a medium heat, stirring occasionally.

4. Now it's time to roll up your breakfast burritos. Lay out one of your wraps, then, in line along the middle of the wrap, spoon on a few tablespoons of beans, some guacamole and some mushrooms, leaving lots of wrap on either side. To roll your burrito, start by folding both ends in, then roll lengthways. Fold the other end of the wrap over or under, while tucking in both ends as you do so. Eat as it is, or put back into the pan for a minute to crisp up the outside. Make the rest of your burritos the same way.

FIVE-MINUTE ONE-PAN GRANOLA

Most people think granola takes ages to make. We wanted to see if it was possible to make it in 5 minutes in one pan, and it turns out it is! This recipe is quick, easy, gluten free and grain free and will keep for months in an airtight jar. Some ideas for how to pimp out your granola – add cacao nibs, goji berries, raisins, sliced dried mango, dates, even freeze-dried raspberries or strawberries.

5
MINS

80g mixed nuts
(almonds/walnuts)

40g desiccated coconut

80g sunflower seeds

40g pumpkin seeds

1 tablespoon chia seeds

2 tablespoons coconut oil

35ml maple syrup

½ teaspoon vanilla extract

a pinch of sea salt

a pinch of ground cinnamon

1. Put the mixed nuts, desiccated coconut, sunflower, pumpkin and chia seeds into a food processor and pulse until all the ingredients are roughly chopped but still have some texture remaining.

2. Put the coconut oil and maple syrup into a large wide-bottomed pan on a high heat until the coconut oil is melted. Stir occasionally to make sure it doesn't burn.

3. Add the nut and seed mixture to the pan, along with the vanilla extract, salt and cinnamon, and mix everything thoroughly. Cook for about 3 minutes, or until the nut mixture starts to colour and brown, making sure you stir continuously.

4. Remove from the heat and leave to cool.

5. When serving, take your granola to the next level by adding some of the extras listed in the intro. You could sprinkle it over porridge, or have it on its own with a splash of non-dairy milk or a dollop of coconut yoghurt.

MEL'S PORRIDGE FOR POWER

This is our friend Mellen's breakfast recipe, complete with her own intro. We love it!

'It's not always easy to fit in all the foods you're supposed to eat these days! This breakfast recipe, which I've been making for a few years in various combinations, comes pretty close to doing it, though. The seeds are packed with protein, calcium and minerals, but they need to be soaked for those nutrients to be absorbed. Turmeric and ginger have anti-inflammatory properties but must have a bit of pepper and oil to work. Seaweed has calcium and other minerals. Depending on the milk you choose, this recipe can be gluten-free and vegan.'

10 MINS

2 teaspoons ground chia seeds

2 teaspoons sesame seeds

1 heaped tablespoon pumpkin seeds

1 heaped tablespoon sunflower seeds

non-dairy milk of choice (almond, rice, oat), or apple juice

dried fruit of choice (e.g. apricots, figs, prunes, dates, mulberries, goji berries, sultanas – ideally unsulphured) (optional)

a small strip of dried dillisk seaweed

For the millet/quinoa porridge

50g millet/quinoa flakes

200ml non-dairy milk of choice

a pinch of ground turmeric

a small pinch of freshly ground black pepper

a pinch of ground cardamom and cinnamon (optional)

1. The night before you want to eat this, soak the ground chia seeds along with the sesame, pumpkin and sunflower seeds in the milk or apple juice and leave overnight in the fridge. If you are using milk, add some dried fruit to the mix to sweeten it up. Cut larger dried fruits like apricots, dates, prunes or figs into smaller pieces before adding. Make sure everything is well covered with milk.

2. Next morning, soak the dillisk seaweed in water and leave aside while you make the porridge.

3. Put the millet/quinoa flakes into a pot and add the milk, along with a pinch of turmeric and ground black pepper. You can add some ground cardamom and cinnamon at this point if you wish. Cook this mixture on a medium heat, stirring continuously until it thickens. Do not let it cook for too long or you will lose the goodness of the turmeric.

4. Drain the water off the seaweed and rinse, then cut into smaller strips with scissors and sprinkle on top of your soaked seeds. Grate in some fresh ginger to taste. Cut up your fresh fruit of choice and scatter on top of the seeds, along with some berries.

a thumb-sized piece of fresh
ginger, peeled

fresh fruit of choice,
including berries

1 teaspoon coconut oil

non-dairy milk of choice, for
pouring over

a drizzle of maple syrup
(optional)

5. Add the coconut oil to the hot porridge and pour
on top of the seed and fruit mixture. Stir everything
together well. Add a little more milk of your choice
and some maple syrup if you like it extra sweet.

ACAI BOWL

This acai bowl is like eating ice cream for breakfast! We use dried acai powder and blueberries to give the striking purple colour. The texture should be thick, so that once you pimp it up, it all sits on the top and does not sink.

10 MINS

3 frozen bananas

250g frozen blueberries

3 tablespoons acai powder

250ml coconut water

3 tablespoons almond butter (cashew or peanut butter work great too)

a selection of toppings (see right for suggestions)

1. Put your bananas, blueberries, acai powder, coconut water and almond butter into a blender and blend until smooth. Pour into a bowl and pimp it up with your choice of the toppings below!

- Fresh berries
- Freshly sliced ripe mango/chopped dried mango
- Freshly sliced kiwi
- Roughly chopped almonds/any other chopped nuts
- Goji berries
- Cacao nibs
- Bee pollen
- Desiccated coconut
- Pistachios

GREEN POWER SMOOTHIE

Bursting with power foods kale, broccoli, ginger, chilli and turmeric, this detoxing smoothie is pretty right on! It also tastes great and will put a real pep in your step. Have it for breakfast or as a meal at any time during the day. It will keep for 3 days in the fridge.

5 MINS

½ a fresh red chilli

½ a fresh pineapple (approx. 300g)

a handful of kale leaves

1 head of broccoli

1 grapefruit

a thumb-size piece of fresh ginger

a thumb-size piece of fresh turmeric/1 teaspoon ground turmeric

½ a ripe avocado

500ml coconut water

cacao nibs and chilli flakes (optional toppings)

1. Chop the end off the chilli, core the pineapple and remove the outer skin, and remove the main centre rib from the kale leaves. Chop the stalk from the head of the broccoli, leaving the florets aside for your dinner (just use the stalk for this recipe).

2. Halve the grapefruit and squeeze the juice into a glass, removing any pips. Peel the ginger and turmeric. Remove the stone from the avocado and scoop the flesh from the skin.

3. Put all the prepared ingredients into a blender with the coconut water and blend until very smooth. Top with cacao nibs and/or chilli flakes, if you are feeling very fiery!

SODA BREAD

Our vegan take on soda bread is easy to make and tasty. Great toasted, with some avocado, lime juice, a sprinkle of chilli flakes and a pinch of sea salt and black pepper.

40 MINS

1 tablespoon ground flax seeds/linseeds (or ground chia seeds)

3 tablespoons water

600g wholemeal flour, plus extra for dusting

1 teaspoon sea salt

2 tablespoons bicarbonate of soda

60g mixed seeds (pumpkin/sunflower/sesame)

350ml almond or rice milk/non-dairy milk of choice

juice of ⅓ of a lemon

1½ tablespoons molasses

1. Preheat the oven to 200°C/400°F/Gas Mark 6. Dust a baking tray with flour.

2. To make your flax egg, combine the ground flax seeds and water in a cup and leave to sit while you mix the dough.

3. Put the flour, salt and bicarbonate of soda into a large bowl and mix slowly with one clean hand, shaped like a claw. Add the seeds and mix through with that same claw-shaped hand.

4. Make a well in the middle of the flour mixture and add about half the milk. Combine with your hand using the same claw technique. Add the flax egg to the bowl along with the lemon juice, the molasses and the remaining milk, and mix right through.

5. Flour your hands and bring your dough together into a round or rectangular shape. Place on the prepared baking tray, scoring an X shape with a knife on the top if you wish. Put the bread into the preheated oven and bake for 25 minutes.

6. Remove from the oven and knock the base of your loaf – if it sounds hollow, it's done! Leave to cool for about 15 minutes.

GLUTEN-FREE BREAD

This loaf was born out of our Happy Heart course, where we created a 100% wholemeal gluten-free loaf based on an Irish porridge bread. Great with some homemade raspberry jam, or toasted, with a big dollop of hummus, tomato and avocado.

75 MINS

1 tablespoon ground flax seeds/linseeds (or ground chia seeds)

3 tablespoons water

1 x 400g soya yoghurt/non-dairy yoghurt of choice

1 tablespoon molasses/sweetener of choice

300g gluten-free oat flakes

2 teaspoons bicarbonate of soda

4 tablespoons mixed seeds (pumpkin/sunflower/sesame)

½ teaspoon sea salt

1. Preheat the oven to 180°C/350°F/Gas Mark 4, and line a 450g or 900g loaf tin with baking parchment.

2. First make your flax egg by combining the ground flax seeds in a cup with the water. Stir and leave to sit for 3-4 minutes.

3. Put the yoghurt, flax egg and molasses into a large mixing bowl and stir well.

4. Mix together the oat flakes, bicarbonate of soda, mixed seeds and salt in a separate bowl. Add to the yoghurt mixture and stir thoroughly. It will be quite a wet batter but will dry out once baked.

5. Tip into the prepared loaf tin and bake in the preheated oven for 1 hour, until risen and nicely browned.

6. As with any bread, leave to cool before slicing.

OYSTER MUSHROOMS WITH GARLIC, TOMATOES & WILTED SPINACH

A super-simple and oh-so-tasty brunch, this is one of our favourites that we constantly go back to. Takes 10 minutes and is so good on toast, with avocado or baked beans.

10 MINS

1 red onion

3 cloves of garlic

150g oyster mushrooms, or other mushrooms

15 cherry tomatoes

1½ tablespoons oil

3 tablespoons tamari/soy sauce

50g baby spinach

a few slices of decent bread (we love sourdough, see page 162)

1 ripe avocado

a pinch of freshly ground black pepper

chilli flakes

1. Peel and finely chop the onion and garlic. Roughly chop the mushrooms and halve the cherry tomatoes.

2. Put a non-stick pan on a high heat and add the oil. Once the oil has heated up, add the onion and garlic to the pan and cook for 2 minutes, stirring regularly.

3. Add the mushrooms and tomatoes and cook for another minute, then add the tamari and cook for a further couple of minutes. Next add the spinach and leave to wilt (it should take less than a minute). Put your bread on to toast, then peel and slice the avocado.

4. Remove the pan from the heat and pile the mixture on to the toast, adding a few slices of avocado. A pinch of black pepper and a sprinkle of chilli flakes top it off perfectly.

5. If you want to take it to the next level, put some hummus on the toast before adding the mushroom mix, and top with a few olives, some kimchi (see pages 150–52), and the avocado and chilli flakes.

FIVE
SIMPLE
SOUPS

RED PEPPER & CASHEW SOUP

This is really tasty, sweet, nourishing and delicious – hard to beat!

30 MINS

2 onions

2 cloves of garlic

2 red peppers

1½ tablespoons oil

1 teaspoon sea salt

150g cashew nuts

1 x 400g tin of chopped tomatoes

1 litre vegetable stock

chilli flakes and coconut milk, to garnish

1. Peel and chop the onions and garlic. Deseed the peppers and chop into small bite-size pieces.

2. Put the oil into a large saucepan over a medium heat. Once hot, add the onions and garlic and cook for 4 minutes, stirring occasionally. Add the chopped peppers and salt, and cook for a further 5 minutes, stirring regularly.

3. Next, add the cashew nuts, tomatoes and stock and turn the heat up high. Bring to the boil, then reduce to a simmer for 15 minutes. Remove from the heat and blend until smooth, using a stick blender.

4. Serve topped with chilli flakes and a drizzle of coconut milk.

LEEK & POTATO SOUP

Super-hearty, nourishing, simple to make, this soup tastes like a big hug on a cold winter's evening!

40 MINS

1 medium onion

3 cloves of garlic

2 large leeks

4 medium potatoes, unpeeled

2 tablespoons oil

2 teaspoons sea salt

1 bay leaf

2 litres vegetable stock

½ teaspoon freshly ground black pepper

juice of ½ a lemon (optional)

black sesame or nigella seeds (optional)

1. Peel and finely slice the onion and garlic. Chop the potatoes and leeks into small bite-size pieces. Make sure you use the full length of the leek, including the green tops – they taste fab and will give the soup that lovely light-green colour.

2. Pour the oil into a large saucepan over a medium heat. Once it heats up, add the onion and garlic and cook for 3 minutes, stirring regularly. Add the potatoes and leeks to the pan, along with the salt and bay leaf, and cook gently for 5 minutes. Add the stock and black pepper, bring to the boil, then reduce the heat to a gentle simmer and cook till the potatoes are nice and soft, about 15 minutes.

3. Remove from the heat and blend with a stick blender until smooth. Taste to see if it needs more salt or pepper, and finish with a squeeze of lemon over each serving and a sprinkle of seeds if you like.

SIMPLE TOMATO SOUP

This tasty soup costs less than €5 for ingredients and takes half an hour to make – exactly what it says in the title!

30 MINS

2 small onions

3 cloves of garlic

2 carrots

2 medium potatoes

2 x 400g tins of chopped tomatoes/800g fresh tomatoes

1½ tablespoons oil

2 teaspoons sea salt

½ teaspoon freshly ground black pepper

1 litre vegetable stock

1 tablespoon maple syrup

a small bunch of fresh basil

To garnish

chilli flakes (optional)

flaked almonds (optional)

1. Peel and finely slice the onions and garlic. Finely slice the carrots and potatoes into equal sized pieces so they cook evenly (no need to peel). Finely dice the tomatoes if using fresh ones.

2. Pour the oil into a large saucepan on a high heat. Once warmed up, add the onions and cook for 1–2 minutes, stirring regularly. Add the garlic and cook for a further minute, stirring occasionally, then add the carrots and potatoes, together with the salt and black pepper, and cook for a further 2 minutes, stirring well.

3. Now add the fresh or tinned tomatoes to the pan with the stock and maple syrup. Bring to the boil, then reduce to a simmer for 15 minutes, or until the potatoes are nice and soft.

4. Pluck the basil leaves from the stalks, keeping a few leaves aside for garnish. Roughly chop the basil leaves and finely chop the stalks, too – there is great flavour in the stalks of most herbs. Add these to the pan, then remove from the heat and blend with a stick blender until smooth.

5. Garnish with chilli flakes and flaked almonds if you like, and the reserved basil leaves, and serve with hunks of decent bread.

SWEET POTATO COCONUT CHILLI SOUP

This soup will leave you wanting more! It's simple, delicious and really hits the spot.

30 MINS

2 small onions

2 cloves of garlic

1 fresh red chilli

2 big sweet potatoes

2 tablespoons oil

1½ teaspoons sea salt

½ teaspoon freshly ground black pepper

1 x 400ml tin of coconut milk

1 litre vegetable stock

To garnish

chilli flakes

fresh basil leaves (optional)

1. Peel and finely chop the onions and garlic. Cut the chilli lengthways and finely chop (remove the seeds if you don't like it too spicy). Chop the sweet potatoes into bite-size pieces – no need to peel, as most of the nutrition is in the skin.

2. Put the oil into a large saucepan over a high heat. Add the onions, chilli and garlic and cook for 1-2 minutes, stirring regularly. Add the sweet potato along with the salt and black pepper, then reduce the heat to medium and leave to cook for 3-5 minutes with the lid on, stirring occasionally.

3. Now add the coconut milk and stock and turn the heat up high. Bring to the boil, then reduce to a simmer for 10-15 minutes, or until the sweet potato is soft and cooked through. Remove from the heat and blend with a stick blender until smooth.

4. Top with chilli flakes and a few basil leaves, if you have them, and serve with decent slices of bread.

CHRISTMAS SOUP

This ultimate Christmas soup is really rich and delicious and will give you that Christmas feeling when you taste it! The vacuum-packed chestnuts are available in most supermarkets around the festive season and will take this soup to the next level, but if you can't get them, simply replace with cashew nuts.

30 MINS

3 small onions

3 cloves of garlic

1 medium sweet potato

2 medium parsnips

2 tablespoons oil

1½ teaspoons sea salt

½ teaspoon freshly ground
   black pepper

10 sprigs of fresh thyme

1½ litres vegetable stock

100g vacuum-packed
   chestnuts

a handful of dried
   cranberries

1. Peel and finely chop the onions and garlic. Roughly chop the sweet potato and the parsnips (no need to peel – the skin is where most of the nutrition is).

2. Put the oil into a large saucepan over a medium heat and, once warmed up, add the onions and garlic. Gently cook for about 5 minutes, stirring regularly.

3. Add the sweet potato, parsnips, salt and black pepper. Remove the leaves from the thyme sprigs and sprinkle in (leaving some aside for garnish). Cook for another 5 minutes. Add the vegetable stock and chestnuts, bring to the boil, then reduce the heat to a gentle simmer for about 15 minutes.

4. Remove from the heat and blend with a stick blender until smooth. Taste and season with more salt and pepper if you think it needs it.

5. Finely slice the dried cranberries and garnish each serving with a sprinkle of these, along with a few of the reserved thyme leaves.

LUNCHES FOR LITTLE ONES

Making wholesome lunches for your little ones is a subject people ask us about all the time. So here are some suggestions for clever ways to get kids to eat their fruit and veg, and some tasty sandwiches packed with goodness!

- First things first – the right-sized containers are essential! And seeing as little mouths only need little portions, getting a few smaller-sized tubs and pots is ideal (it also means less waste).

- Our kids thankfully love the bright colours of veg like red peppers, carrots and cucumber, so a frequent lunch contender simply involves cutting them up into baby batons and pairing them with a tub of hummus. Alongside this we'll cut a toasted wholemeal pitta bread pocket into little soldiers. And finally add a Medjool date and some fruit, so a sweet tooth is satisfied with something other than jellies!

- Steve's daughter May looooves tahini (which is great, seeing as lots of schools are going nut-free). A great lunch option for her is spreading some tahini on a rice cake, mushing a banana over that, popping another rice cake on top and – tah-dah! – you've got a tasty little sambo. Fill a little tub with blueberry soya yoghurt and pop in an energy ball and a mandarin (peeled – you want to make it as easy as possible for your kids to eat healthily), and that's lunch sorted.

- You can pick up packets of falafel in most supermarkets/health food shops these days, so another popular lunch option involves just heating those up and popping them into a lunchbox beside some toasted pitta soldiers, with a little hummus in a tub. Add some berries in another tub. Simple, but delicious.

- Last night's leftover veggie chilli can be a great option for the kids' lunch. Cooking a bit of wholemeal couscous to accompany this will take about 4 minutes, and then all you have to do is get your tight-seal Tupperware, a piece of fruit and you're done!

- Some homemade soup is also lovely during the winter months, so we'd definitely recommend investing in a little flask and pairing the soup with some wholemeal bread for a super-easy and nutritious lunch.

THREE PLANT-BASED BACK-TO-SCHOOL SANDWICHES

We grew up bringing ham and cheese sandwiches to school every day but times have changed, and sandwich fillings can be so much more interesting these days! Here are three easy back-to-school sandwiches. The first two are super-tasty fillings that you can make at the start of the week and alternate on different days. The third is our vegan take on a classic. With all these recipes, use a good-quality wholewheat or sourdough bread to assemble your sandwiches.

— MAKES ENOUGH FILLING FOR 4 DECENT SANDWICHES —

VEGAN CHICK'N TIKKA MASALA

15 MINS

3 cloves of garlic

300g block of tempeh/seitan

1 x 400ml tin of coconut milk

1 tablespoon ground cumin

1 tablespoon paprika

1 teaspoon smoked paprika

1 teaspoon ground ginger

½ teaspoon chilli powder

½ teaspoon freshly ground black pepper

1 tablespoon maple syrup

100g tomato purée

1 tablespoon tamari/soy sauce

1 teaspoon sea salt

oil, for frying

1. Peel and finely chop the garlic. Finely slice the tempeh into small strips and set aside in a bowl. Put the garlic and all the remaining ingredients, apart from the oil, into a blender and blend until smooth. Pour this mixture over the tempeh and leave to marinate for as long as you have – ideally overnight, but 5 minutes will do too!

2. Put 1 tablespoon of oil into a non-stick pan on a high heat, add the tempeh strips and cook for 3–5 minutes, turning regularly until golden. Remove from the heat and it's good to go!

3. Serve in a sandwich with salad leaves, avocado, kimchi (see pages 151–52) and some vegan coleslaw (see page 139).

VEGAN EGG MAYO

10 MINS

1 x 400g tin of chickpeas

½ a red onion

4 scallions

100g gherkins/pickles

4 tablespoons vegan
  mayonnaise (see page 138)

1 tablespoon Dijon/
  wholegrain mustard

1 tablespoon apple cider
  vinegar

juice of 1 lime

½ teaspoon freshly ground
  black pepper

1. Drain and rinse the chickpeas and put into a mixing bowl. Smash them with a potato masher or fork until they are broken up but still have some texture. Peel and finely chop the red onion, finely slice the scallions, and add both to the chickpeas. Finely chop the gherkins and add these too, along with all the remaining ingredients. Mix everything together well.

2. Serve on wholewheat bread, with some Dijon or spicy brown mustard, cos lettuce/rocket leaves and a few slices of tomato.

VEGAN SAUSAGE WITH VEGAN MAYO

10 MINS

1 tablespoon oil

6 Linda McCartney
  vegetarian sausages

2 tablespoons tomato
  ketchup (see page 138)

2 tablespoons vegan mayo
  (see page138)

a few slices of tomato

a few cos lettuce leaves/a
  handful of rocket leaves

1. Put the oil into a non-stick pan and cook the sausages until golden. Slice them in half lengthways.

2. Slather the ketchup on one slice of bread and the mayo on the other. Put the sausages on, add a couple of slices of tomato and sprinkle on your leaves of choice. Sandwich together and enjoy cold or toasted.

SUPER
QUICK
DINNERS

CHICKPEA & AUBERGINE CURRY

Quick, tasty, satisfying . . . there is not a lot else to say about this dish! Great served with some toasted wholemeal pittas chopped into soldiers and some brown rice as a side. Well worth a shot.

20 MINS

1 onion

3 cloves of garlic

a thumb-size piece of fresh ginger

½ a fresh red chilli

1 aubergine

1½ tablespoons oil

3 tablespoons tamari/ soy sauce

5 tablespoons water

1 x 400g tin of chickpeas

a small bunch of fresh coriander, basil or chives

2 tablespoons curry powder

1 x 400ml tin of coconut milk

1 x 400g tin of chopped tomatoes

juice of ½ a lemon

1 teaspoon freshly ground black pepper

chilli flakes, to garnish

1. Peel and finely chop the onion, garlic and ginger. Remove the end of the chilli and the seeds, if you don't like it spicy, and finely chop. Chop the aubergine into small pieces (we like using a serrated knife for this, as it's best for chopping aubergines).

2. Put a large saucepan on a high heat, add the oil and leave it to heat up for a minute. Add the onion, garlic, ginger and chilli and cook for 2½ minutes, stirring regularly.

3. Add the aubergine and the tamari and cook for 5 minutes, continuing to stir well so that all the aubergine gets infused with the lovely flavour. Now add the water and cook for a further 3-4 minutes. The aubergine should be soft and cooked through.

4. In the meantime, drain the chickpeas and rinse thoroughly. Roughly chop the coriander, basil or chives, reserving some for the garnish. Add these, along with the curry powder, coconut milk, chopped tomatoes, lemon juice and black pepper, to the pan and cook for 5 minutes. Bring to the boil, then reduce the heat and simmer for 1 further minute.

5. Remove from the heat, taste and adjust the seasoning if you need to. Garnish each serving with the reserved chopped coriander, basil or chives and, if you like it spicy, some chilli flakes.

CHICKPEA TIKKA MASALA

Chicken tikka masala has been called the UK's national dish, originating when a chef added tomato soup to a curry to make it less spicy! Our version, based on chickpeas, is rich, creamy, and lovely and 'meaty'!

15 MINS

For the paste

1 tablespoon cumin seeds

1 tablespoon coriander seeds

2 cloves of garlic

a thumb-size piece of fresh ginger

½ a fresh red chilli

a bunch of fresh coriander

1 heaped teaspoon garam masala

½ teaspoon smoked paprika

1½ teaspoons sea salt

½ teaspoon freshly ground black pepper

1 tablespoon tomato purée

1 x 400g tin of chopped tomatoes

For the curry

3 scallions

300g mushrooms (we love oyster, but any mushrooms will do)

1½ tablespoons oil

2 x 400g tins of chickpeas

1 x 400ml tin of coconut milk

juice of ½ a lime

chilli flakes (optional)

1. In a dry frying pan, fry the cumin and coriander seeds for 3–5 minutes on a high heat until the cumin seeds start to pop, stirring regularly. Peel the garlic and ginger.

2. To make your paste, whiz together the garlic, ginger, chilli, the stalks from the fresh coriander (setting the leaves aside for later), the garam masala, smoked paprika, salt, pepper, tomato purée, chopped tomatoes and the toasted cumin and coriander seeds in a blender until smooth.

3. Chop the scallions into small slices and cut the mushrooms into small bite-size pieces. Put the oil into a large frying pan over a high heat, and once the pan and oil are hot, add the mushrooms and fry for 3–4 minutes. If the mushrooms start to stick, add a few tablespoons of the paste.

4. Drain the chickpeas, rinse thoroughly and add to the pan together with the chopped scallions, the rest of the paste and the coconut milk. Bring to the boil, then reduce the heat to a simmer and cook for a further 2 minutes.

5. Squeeze in the lime juice, taste, and season with more salt, pepper and maybe some chilli flakes if you think it needs it. Chop the reserved coriander leaves roughly and sprinkle over each serving as a garnish.

6. Lovely served with soya yoghurt and toasted almond flakes on top.

SWEET ALMOND & LIME CURRY

This is a super-tasty and delicious dish that presents really well. It's quick to make and full of flavour. We serve it with wholemeal couscous, but it works great with noodles if that's your preference.

15 MINS

a thumb-size piece of fresh ginger

3 cloves of garlic

4 scallions

1 fresh red chilli/ 1 teaspoon chilli flakes

200g mushrooms (we like chestnut mushrooms)

1 courgette

1 red pepper

200g wholemeal couscous/4 nests of noodles (200g)

1 teaspoon sea salt

3 tablespoons oil

1 x 400ml tin of coconut milk

2 tablespoons tamari/soy sauce

juice of 1 lime

3 tablespoons almond butter

2 tablespoons curry powder

1 tablespoon maple syrup

a handful of sugarsnap peas/baby spinach

1. Peel and finely chop the ginger and garlic. Finely chop the scallions and chilli (removing the seeds from the chilli if you don't like it spicy). Chop the mushrooms into bite-size pieces, along with the courgette and deseeded red pepper.

2. Boil the kettle for the couscous/noodles. If using couscous, put it into a large bowl, add a pinch of salt and a tablespoon of oil, and mix through. Pour boiling water in until the water level goes just above the top of the couscous and leave it to sit for 5 minutes with a plate on top. If using noodles, cook as per the instructions on the back of the packet, then drain and rinse.

3. Pour 2 tablespoons of oil into a large frying pan or wok over a high heat. Once the pan is hot, add the ginger, garlic, scallions and chilli and cook for 2 minutes, stirring regularly.

4. Now add the mushrooms, courgette and red pepper along with the salt and cook for 3 minutes, stirring regularly. Pour in the coconut milk, tamari and lime juice, and continue to stir regularly.

5. In a bowl mix the almond butter and 150ml of boiling water, using a fork, and add to the pan along with the curry powder and the maple syrup (the syrup will balance the heat of the chilli and curry powder). Bring to the boil, then reduce to a gentle simmer for 3–5 minutes.

6. Roughly chop your sugarsnap peas/spinach and mix through the curry a minute before turning off the heat.

7. If using couscous, fluff it up. Roughly chop the coriander. Serve each portion with some couscous/noodles, with the curry on top, and garnish with coriander and almonds if you like.

EASY THREE-BEAN SWEET POTATO & COCONUT CURRY

A really simple curry that is perfect as a midweek dinner. Goes well with wholemeal couscous, noodles or any grain of choice. The precooked brown rice/quinoa that is now available in sachets in supermarkets works great here too.

15 MINS

1 x 400g tin of butter beans

1 x 400g tin of black beans

1 x 400ml tin of chickpeas

1 red onion

2 cloves of garlic

1 courgette

100g sweet potato

½ a carrot

1½ tablespoons oil

1½ teaspoons sea salt

400ml vegetable stock

1 x 400ml tin of coconut milk

2 tablespoons curry powder

juice of ½ a lemon

1 tablespoon tamari/soy sauce

a handful of baby spinach

To garnish

½ teaspoon chilli flakes

pink peppercorns

a handful of cashew nuts, toasted

1. Drain all the different beans and rinse thoroughly. Peel and finely chop the onion and garlic. Chop the courgette into bite-size pieces. Grate the sweet potato and carrot – no need to peel.

2. Put the oil into a medium pan over a high heat. Once the oil is hot, add the onion and garlic and cook for 1 minute, stirring regularly until softening. Add the courgette along with the salt, grated sweet potato and carrot and cook for 3 minutes, stirring continuously.

3. Add the vegetable stock, coconut milk, beans and curry powder to the pan and bring to the boil, then reduce the heat to a gentle simmer for a further 3 minutes.

4. Now stir in the lemon juice, tamari and spinach and cook for another couple of minutes, until the spinach has wilted.

5. Remove from the heat. Taste and add more sea salt or some black pepper if you think it needs it. Top with chilli flakes, pink peppercorns and toasted cashews.

CAULIFLOWER & PEA KORMA

Dave went to Punjab in India a few years back and ate some of the best kormas he has ever had! Here is his take on a quick-fire cauliflower and pea korma. The cauliflower gives it a nice bite and goes really well with the creamy tomato curry sauce. Lovely served with brown rice. You can substitute broccoli for the cauliflower, if you prefer.

15 MINS

250g frozen peas

3 cloves of garlic

a thumb-size piece of fresh ginger

½ a fresh red chilli

4 scallions

1 head of cauliflower/ broccoli

1 large red pepper

1½ tablespoons oil

1 teaspoon cumin seeds

1 x 400ml tin of coconut milk

1 x 400g tin of chopped tomatoes

1½ tablespoons curry powder

½ teaspoon freshly ground black pepper

1½ teaspoons sea salt

1 tablespoon maple syrup

juice of ½ a lime

To garnish

a small bunch of fresh coriander

flaked almonds

chilli flakes

1. Put the frozen peas into a bowl of boiling water to thaw.

2. Peel and finely chop the garlic and ginger. Finely slice the chilli, removing the seeds if you don't like it too spicy. Finely slice the scallions. Cut the cauliflower/broccoli florets off the stalk and chop them into small bite-size pieces. Deseed and finely chop the red pepper.

3. Put the oil into a large pan over a high heat. Once the pan is hot, add the garlic, ginger, chilli and scallions and cook for 1½ minutes, stirring regularly.

4. Next, add the cauliflower/broccoli, red pepper and cumin seeds and cook for 2 minutes, stirring regularly. Drain the peas and add these along with the remaining korma ingredients, bring to the boil, then reduce to a simmer for 2 minutes.

5. Remove from the heat. Roughly chop the coriander and sprinkle over each serving, along with some flaked almonds and our old favourite – chilli flakes!

GO-TO DAHL

Amazing the flavours that can be developed in ten minutes! We spent quite a while tweaking this recipe and reckon we've got it spot on - smooth, creamy, spicy and very nourishing. The dahl works great served with toasted wholemeal pitta bread chopped into soldiers, or else with wholemeal couscous.

10 MINS

3 cloves of garlic

a thumb-size piece of fresh ginger

4 scallions

1 x 400g tin of chickpeas

1 x 400g tin of cooked lentils (we usually use green ones)

10–15 cherry tomatoes

1 tablespoon oil

a handful of baby spinach

1 x 400ml tin of coconut milk

juice of ½ a lime

2 tablespoons curry powder

2 teaspoons ground cumin

1 teaspoon sea salt

1 tablespoon tamari/soy sauce

½ teaspoon freshly ground black pepper

To serve

3 wholemeal pitta breads

chilli flakes

a small bunch of fresh coriander or other fresh herb of choice

1. Peel and finely chop the garlic and ginger. Finely chop the scallions. Drain the chickpeas and lentils and rinse thoroughly. Chop the cherry tomatoes in half.

2. Heat the oil for 1 minute in a large saucepan over a high heat. Add the garlic, ginger and scallions and cook for 1 minute. Add the cherry tomatoes and cook for a further 2 minutes. Add the remaining ingredients to the pan and bring to the boil, stirring occasionally to make sure it doesn't stick to the bottom. Leave to simmer for a further 2 minutes, then take off the heat.

3. While the dahl is simmering, toast your pitta breads.

4. Garnish with some chilli flakes and fresh coriander (or other fresh herb of your choice), and serve with your hot pittas, chopped into soldiers, and some rice or couscous.

INDONESIAN SATAY

This lovely rich, creamy, fresh and nutty dish with crunchy veg and fresh coriander will be ready to eat in 15 minutes. We used courgette, red pepper and tinned chickpeas here, but you can replace them with any of your favourite fast-cooking veg, such as mushrooms, sugarsnap peas or spinach.

15 MINS

½ a thumb-size piece of fresh ginger

2 cloves of garlic

4 scallions

½ a fresh red chilli

1 red pepper

1 courgette

1 x 400g tin of chickpeas

1 tablespoon oil

2 tablespoons tamari/soy sauce

4 tablespoons peanut butter/almond butter

2 tablespoons apple cider vinegar

2 tablespoons maple syrup/ other liquid sweetener

350ml warm water

sea salt and freshly ground black pepper

To garnish

1 small bunch of fresh coriander or basil

1 pack of beansprouts

a handful of toasted nuts

1. Peel and finely chop the ginger and garlic. Finely slice the scallions. Deseed and finely slice the chilli and the red pepper (leave the seeds in the chilli if you like it spicy). Finely chop the courgette. Drain the chickpeas and rinse thoroughly.

2. Put a medium-size saucepan on a high heat and add the oil. Once the oil is hot, add the garlic, ginger, chilli and scallions and cook for 1½ minutes on a high heat, stirring regularly.

3. Next, add the chopped courgette and red pepper and cook for another minute. Add the tamari, cook for another minute, then turn the heat down to low/medium.

4. Put the peanut butter, apple cider vinegar, maple syrup and 150ml of the warm water into a blender and whiz until smooth (or whisk vigorously with a fork), then add to the pan.

5. Slowly add the remaining water, along with the chickpeas, and turn the heat back up to high. Bring to the boil, then remove from the heat and season with salt and pepper to your taste.

6. Divide between four bowls, topping each serving with roughly chopped fresh coriander or basil, fresh red chilli and some beansprouts. Toasted nuts go great as a garnish, too.

ONE-POT SPAG BOL

A lovely quick take on spaghetti bolognese that is cooked all together in one pot – yes, you did read that right, pasta and sauce all cooked in the same pot! It works really well and is quick, tasty and creamy. Nutritional yeast is a condiment that is very common in vegan circles – it has a cheesy taste without any of the saturated fat and is available in most health food stores.

20 MINS

1 red onion

4 cloves of garlic

1 carrot

1 stick of celery

1 fresh green chilli

a handful of cherry tomatoes

1 x 400g tin of cooked lentils

1 tablespoon olive oil

sea salt and freshly ground
  black pepper

1.2 litres vegetable stock

1 x 400g tin of chopped
  tomatoes

400g wholemeal spaghetti

juice of ½ a lemon

2 tablespoons tamari/soy
  sauce

a decent bunch of fresh basil

nutritional yeast, to serve

1. Peel and finely chop the onion and garlic. Grate the carrot, thinly slice the celery and chop the chilli into small pieces. Cut the cherry tomatoes in half. Drain and rinse the lentils.

2. Put 1 tablespoon of oil into a large pot (big enough to take the spaghetti) over a high heat. Once the oil heats up, add the onion, garlic, carrot, celery, chilli and a good pinch of salt. Cook for 3 minutes, stirring regularly.

3. Next, add all the rest of the ingredients except the basil and nutritional yeast (you may need to break the spaghetti to fit it into your pot). Bring to the boil, then reduce to a simmer and cook until the pasta is ready – wholemeal spaghetti normally takes about 9–11 minutes, depending on the brand. Remove the pot from the heat.

4. Pluck the basil leaves from their stalks and set aside. Chop the stalks finely and add to the pot.

5. Garnish with the basil leaves, sprinkle with the nutritional yeast and serve.

ONE-POT CREAMY TOMATO PASTA

Easy, tasty and very little clean-up! It's a great midweek dinner that also works well as a cold salad the next day if you make extra. We love to serve this with a hunk of crusty bread to clean up the juices left on the plate.

20 MINS

1 onion

3 cloves of garlic

1 aubergine

150g mushrooms of your choice

1½ tablespoons oil

4 tablespoons tamari/soy sauce

100ml water

2 x 400g tins of chopped tomatoes

100g tomato purée

1 tablespoon maple syrup

½ teaspoon freshly ground black pepper

500ml vegetable stock

500ml non-dairy milk (we use oat milk)

500g wholemeal pasta (use gluten-free if you prefer)

2 tablespoons nutritional yeast (optional)

To garnish

a small bunch of fresh basil

chilli flakes

a little nutritional yeast

1. Peel and finely chop the onion and garlic. Slice the aubergine into small bite-size pieces and finely chop the mushrooms.

2. Put a large saucepan on a high heat and fry the onion and garlic in the oil for 2 minutes, stirring regularly until they start to brown. Add the aubergine and mushrooms and cook for 3-4 minutes. Add the tamari and cook until it has all been absorbed or evaporated (about 2 minutes), then pour in the water and cook for a further 5 minutes. Both the aubergine and the mushrooms should be soft and super-tasty by now.

3. Add the tinned tomatoes, tomato purée, maple syrup and black pepper and mix well. Stir in the stock and non-dairy milk, finally adding the pasta. If using spaghetti, break it up so that it all fits into the pan and is submerged in the liquid. Mix well.

4. Once it starts to boil, reduce the heat and leave to simmer so that the liquid starts to evaporate. Every so often, use a wooden spoon to gently mix through the pasta, making sure it doesn't stick together.

5. Once the sauce is reduced and the pasta is cooked (check the packet for the cooking time), add the nutritional yeast (if using). Taste and add more salt if needed.

6. Tear the basil leaves roughly and sprinkle them over each serving, along with some chilli flakes, more nutritional yeast (and some grated cheese if you fancy it).

LOWER-FAT PESTO 'PASTA'

We love pesto! Often people forget how easy it is to make and how tasty it can be when made fresh. Here we use half oil and half water, to make the pesto lower in fat while keeping its great flavour. We often serve this with sliced fresh red chilli/dried chilli flakes, cherry tomatoes or even pink peppercorns. To make it speedy, we've used wholewheat noodles instead of pasta, as the noodles cook in half the time, but if you have the time and prefer pasta, simply use that instead.

10 MINS

4 nests of dried whole-wheat noodles (200g)

a handful of cherry tomatoes (different coloured ones, ideally)

For the basil pesto

3 cloves of garlic

75ml water

75ml neutral-tasting olive oil/ sunflower oil

1 teaspoon sea salt

juice of ½ a lime

100g roasted cashew nuts

50g fresh basil

To garnish

sliced fresh red chilli/ chilli flakes

pink peppercorns

1. Fill and boil a kettle for the noodles and gather your ingredients for the pesto. Pour the boiled water into a medium-size pot and cook the noodles as per the instructions on the pack (4 minutes). Cut the cherry tomatoes into halves or quarters.

2. While the noodles are boiling, make your pesto. Peel the garlic and put it into a blender or food processor together with the rest of the pesto ingredients, apart from the basil. If using a normal blender, first separate the basil leaves from the stalks before adding them. If you have a high-speed blender, use both the leaves and the stalks of the basil. Blend until smooth.

3. When ready, drain and rinse the noodles, then transfer them to a frying pan or a large pot together with all the pesto. Mix well, so the pesto is evenly spread through the noodles. Add the cherry tomatoes and warm through gently.

4. When serving, garnish with sliced fresh red chilli/ chilli flakes and pink peppercorns for a colourful effect.

ONE-POT CREAMY MUSHROOM PASTA

This one-pot wonder is really quick and super-easy, perfect for midweek or for when you are in a rush. It's surprising how well the pasta cooks in the sauce, and how creamy and cheesy it tastes without any cream or cheese! If you don't want to use wine, just replace it with the same amount of vegetable stock.

20 MINS

1 medium red onion

2 cloves of garlic

400g mushrooms

2 tablespoons oil

200ml white wine

a small handful of fresh thyme sprigs

500g wholemeal/spelt spaghetti

800ml oat milk (or other non-dairy milk)

500ml vegetable stock

2 teaspoons sea salt

2 tablespoons nutritional yeast, plus a little for garnish

juice of ½ a lemon

freshly ground black pepper

chilli flakes (optional)

1. Peel and finely chop the onion and garlic. Chop the mushrooms reasonably finely.

2. Pour the oil into a large pan (big enough to take the pasta later) on a high heat, and add your chopped onion and garlic. Cook until they start to brown, about 2–3 minutes, stirring continuously. Add the chopped mushrooms and cook for 2 minutes.

3. Add the wine and most of the thyme leaves (leaving a couple of sprigs aside), and cook for another minute.

4. Break the spaghetti into the pan and add the oat milk, stock and salt. Turn up the heat and cover the pan with a lid. Once the sauce starts to boil, take the lid off so that the liquid starts to evaporate. Every so often, take a wooden spoon and gently stir the pasta, making sure it doesn't stick together. When the sauce has reduced and the pasta is cooked, add the nutritional yeast and the lemon juice.

5. Remove from the heat, taste and season with more salt, if you think it needs it, and some black pepper. Top each serving with a few sprigs of thyme, a little more nutritional yeast, and chilli flakes if you like a bit of spice.

QUESADILLAS

Simple, quick and satisfying, a quesadilla is based around a hot tortilla folded over with cheese (queso), which sticks it all together. Here, we charred some sweetcorn to give it extra flavour and bite, and made it into a lovely salsa with black beans. Along with some avocado and vegan cheese, it's turned into this delicious Mexican snack!

15 MINS

1 x 250g tin of sweetcorn

1 x 400g tin of black beans

1 fresh red chilli

20 cherry tomatoes (different coloured ones, ideally)

1 tablespoon oil

1 tablespoon ground cumin

1 teaspoon ground coriander

juice of 1 lime

½ teaspoon sea salt

a bunch of fresh coriander

1 ripe avocado

1 x 200g pack of vegan cheese or 1 x nacho cheese (see page 141)

4 wholemeal/corn tortillas or wraps

1. Drain the sweetcorn and black beans separately, and rinse thoroughly. Chop the chilli finely, removing the seeds if you want it less spicy. Chop the cherry tomatoes into quarters.

2. Put 1 tablespoon of oil on to a griddle or into a frying pan on a high heat. Add the sweetcorn and cook until it starts to char slightly (3-4 minutes). Next, add the black beans, chilli, cumin, coriander, half the lime juice, the cherry tomatoes and the salt and cook for a further 3 minutes. While cooking, use the back of a wooden spoon to mash the beans so that they break up - they will hold the salsa together.

3. Chop the fresh coriander roughly and stir half of it into the pan. Remove the salsa from the heat and transfer to a bowl. Cut the avocado in half and slice lengthways while still in the skin. Using a spoon, remove the slices from the skin into another small bowl. Grate the cheese into another bowl, or if using nacho cheese have it ready to spread. Give the griddle/frying pan a quick wash.

4. Put the dry pan back on a high heat and put in a tortilla. Add a generous handful of grated cheese or 2 tablespoons of nacho cheese and spread it around the tortilla. Add a serving of salsa, a few slices of avocado, and finish with another handful of cheese or a dollop of nacho cheese. Once the tortilla or wrap starts to brown, fold it in half so it becomes a half circle. Wait until the cheese starts to melt and stick it together.

5. Remove from the heat and slice in two. Repeat till you have made enough. Eat while hot!

QUICK-FIRE BURRITOS

Quick, satisfying and delivers on taste . . . this is a crowd-pleaser! Here you are making four components and layering up a super flavour-packed burrito. Great for lunch, dinner or even a spicy brunch.

15 MINS

4 wholewheat wraps

For the couscous

1 clove of garlic

a pinch of chilli flakes

1 teaspoon ground cumin

½ teaspoon smoked paprika

½ teaspoon sea salt

200g wholewheat couscous

250ml boiling water

For the refried beans

2 cloves of garlic

1 x 100g tin of sweetcorn

1 x 400g tin of black beans/
 kidney beans

1 tablespoon oil

2 teaspoons ground cumin

2 tablespoons tamari/soy
 sauce

½ a bunch of fresh coriander

juice of 1 lime

For the salsa

2 cloves of garlic

4 scallions

1. Peel and finely chop the garlic and put it into a large serving dish with the chilli flakes, cumin, smoked paprika, salt and couscous. Mix around and pour on enough boiling water to come about 2cm above the dry couscous. Cover with a lid and leave to sit for 5 minutes.

2. To make the refried beans, peel and roughly slice the garlic, drain and rinse the sweetcorn, then drain the beans and rinse thoroughly until the water runs clear. Put the oil into a frying pan on a high heat, then add the garlic. Add the sweetcorn and cook for 3 minutes, until it starts to char slightly. Add the beans, together with the cumin and tamari. Roughly chop the coriander leaves, finely chop the stalks, and pop both leaves and stalks into the pan. Remove from the heat, add the lime juice and give it all a good stir. Once all is well mixed, use the back of a wooden spoon to mash the beans and set aside.

3. Now make your salsa. Peel and finely chop the garlic and finely slice the scallions. Deseed and finely chop the chilli (leave the seeds in if you want it spicy). Put these into a medium-size bowl along with the chopped tomatoes, salt, maple syrup and lime juice. Chop the coriander, stalks included, and mix this through as well.

4. To make the yoghurt dressing, spoon the yoghurt into a bowl and add the lime juice and maple syrup. Mix well with a fork.

1 fresh red chilli

1 x 400g tin of chopped tomatoes

½ teaspoon sea salt

1 teaspoon maple syrup

juice of ½ a lime

½ a bunch of fresh coriander

For the yoghurt dressing

250g soya/coconut yoghurt, or other yoghurt of choice

juice of ½ a lime

1 tablespoon maple syrup

5. Time to assemble your burritos! Spoon a generous serving of each filling into your wholewheat wrap, then roll up and enjoy. To roll your burrito, simply fold in the ends slightly and start rolling from one of the sides. Keep rolling until it is compact and rolled up tightly. If you like your burrito warm, once wrapped, put it back into a hot dry pan for a minute on each side to toast and crisp up.

THREE-BEAN CHILLI

A super-fast, easy and well-balanced dinner, this chilli's a real winner. Great served with short-grain brown rice. Because this is such a fast-cooking dish, it makes sense to use pre-cooked brown rice or quinoa (available in sachets from most supermarkets) – that way it will all be ready in time.

10 MINS

3 cloves of garlic

1 fresh red chilli

1 yellow pepper

a bunch of scallions

1 x 400g tin of kidney beans

1 x 400g tin of butter beans

1 x 400g tin of black beans/chickpeas

2 tablespoons oil

2 x 400g tins of chopped tomatoes

6 tablespoons tomato purée (100g)

1 tablespoon maple syrup

2 teaspoons ground cumin

2 teaspoons ground coriander

2 tablespoons tamari/soy sauce

½ teaspoon smoked paprika

juice of 1 lime

1 teaspoon sea salt

½ teaspoon freshly ground black pepper

To serve

fresh coriander or chives

avocado (optional)

natural plain soya yoghurt

chilli flakes

1. Peel and finely chop the garlic. Finely slice the chilli, removing the seeds if you don't like it spicy. Deseed the yellow pepper and finely chop. Finely slice the scallions, and drain and rinse the beans/chickpeas.

2. Put the oil into a large saucepan over a high heat. Once the pan is hot, add the garlic, chilli, yellow pepper and scallions, and cook for 2½ minutes, stirring regularly.

3. Now add all the remaining ingredients and bring to the boil, stirring regularly. Remove from the heat and serve with chopped fresh coriander or chives, some sliced avocado (if you have it) and/or natural plain soya yoghurt, topping it all with some chilli flakes.

STUFFED SWEET POTATO SKINS

This is a very tasty and satisfying dinner that will brighten up your evening and fill your kitchen with sweet Mexican aromas! Although it takes a bit of time to bake the potatoes, you can do this ahead, so there's only 10 minutes' actual preparation time. A bit borderline for a quick dinners section, but delicious!

80 MINS

5 medium sweet potatoes (1.8kg)

1 x 400g tin of black beans

1 x 100g tin of sweetcorn

1 fresh red chilli

3 scallions

2 cloves of garlic

a small bunch of fresh coriander

2 teaspoons ground cumin

1 teaspoon paprika

juice of 1 lime

2 teaspoons sea salt

½ teaspoon freshly ground black pepper

1 large ripe avocado

1. Preheat the oven to 180°C/350°F/Gas Mark 4.

2. Scrub the sweet potatoes, leaving the skin on, then cut the ends off and cut into halves lengthways. Once the oven is heated, put the sweet potatoes on a baking tray and roast for about 1 hour (they are ready when you insert a fork and the flesh comes out easily). Remove from the oven, leaving it on, and allow to cool for 5-10 minutes.

3. When cool, scoop out the sweet potato flesh and place in a large mixing bowl. Scoop carefully - try to leave a thin layer around the skin so that each half can hold its shape. Place the skins back on the tray, cut side up, then return to the oven and bake for a further 10 minutes, allowing them to get nice and crispy.

4. While the skins are baking in the oven, mash the sweet potato flesh that you scooped out. Drain and rinse the black beans and sweetcorn. Deseed and finely chop the chilli, chop the scallions and add them both to the mixing bowl. Peel and finely chop the garlic, chop the coriander and add them to the bowl with the black beans and sweetcorn. Add the cumin, paprika, lime juice, salt and black pepper and mix thoroughly.

5. Once the skins are done, remove from the oven and fill each skin with sweet potato mixture. Pop back into the oven for a further 5 minutes, to heat and crisp the tops. Serve with slices of avocado on top. Lovely topped with vegan mayo and sprinkled with extra coriander, as in the picture.

THAI GOLDEN CURRY WITH NOODLES

This is our take on a fast-cooking Thai yellow curry, with noodles already in it! It's quick and easy, ideal for midweek and super-tasty, too.

20 MINS

a pinch of sea salt

4 nests of dried wholewheat noodles (200g – use buckwheat or brown rice noodles for a gluten-free option)

3 cloves of garlic

a thumb-size piece of fresh ginger

1 fresh red chilli

1 yellow pepper

1 courgette

4 scallions

1 head of broccoli

1½ tablespoons oil

1 x 400ml tin of coconut milk

1 tablespoon maple syrup

juice of 1 lime

3 tablespoons tamari/soy sauce

2 teaspoons ground turmeric

½ teaspoon freshly ground black pepper

To serve

a small bunch of fresh coriander or basil

toasted sesame seeds

chilli flakes

pickled red onions (see page 148)

1. Bring a small pot of water to the boil with a pinch of salt, add the noodles and cook as per the instructions on the pack. Drain, rinse in a colander and set aside over the sink.

2. Peel and finely chop the garlic and ginger. Chop the end off the chilli and finely slice, removing the seeds if you don't like it spicy. Deseed the pepper and finely chop, along with the courgette. Finely slice the scallions, then chop the florets off the broccoli stalk and cut them into bite-size pieces.

3. Put a wide-bottomed pan (such as a wok) on a high heat, add the oil and leave to heat up for 1 minute. Add the garlic, ginger and chilli and cook for another minute, stirring regularly.

4. Next, add the yellow pepper, courgette, scallions and broccoli florets and cook for 2 minutes. Add the coconut milk, maple syrup, lime juice, tamari, turmeric and black pepper, then the noodles, and cook for a further 3 minutes.

5. Remove from the heat. Roughly chop the coriander or basil and divide between the servings, along with the toasted sesame seeds, chilli flakes and some pickled red onions.

MASSAMAN CURRY

Our tasty take on the Thai classic, this dish goes great served in a bowl with some wholewheat noodles or brown rice. You can add chopped fresh coriander to the garnish if you like.

20 MINS

For the paste/sauce

3 cloves of garlic

a thumb-size piece of fresh ginger

½ a fresh red chilli (keep the other half for garnish)

1 stalk of lemongrass

200ml vegetable stock

1 x 400ml tin of coconut milk

1 tablespoon maple syrup

½ tablespoon almond butter

1 teaspoon cumin seeds

1 teaspoon coriander seeds

1 teaspoon ground cinnamon

juice of ½ a lemon

1 tablespoon oil

For the curry

1 x 300g block of tofu/tempeh or 250g mushrooms

4 scallions

1 red pepper

1 yellow pepper

1 head of pak choi

2 tablespoons oil

3 tablespoons tamari/soy sauce

1. Peel and chop the garlic and ginger. Cut the chilli in half and set one half aside for the garnish. Remove the outer leaves of the lemongrass, trim the dried top third and the bottom nub off and roughly chop the rest. Then put all the paste/sauce ingredients into a blender and blend till smooth.

2. Cut the tofu into small cubes or chop the mushrooms. Finely chop the scallions and peppers. Chop the nub off the end of the pak choi and chop the rest into bite-size pieces.

3. Put the oil into a large pan over a high heat. When hot, add the tofu or mushrooms and cook for 1 minute, stirring regularly. Add the tamari and cook for a further 3 minutes, stirring occasionally.

4. Add the scallions and peppers to the pan, together with 4 tablespoons of the paste/sauce, and cook for 2 minutes. Add the rest of the paste and the pak choi, and stir well. When it boils, remove from the heat.

SOME SERVING IDEAS

This dish is lovely garnished with finely sliced fresh red chillies, sprinkled over each serving, along with sesame seeds, chopped scallions and coriander.

SHIITAKE, GINGER & SESAME PAD THAI

A simple, super-tasty dinner that really delivers in flavour. Use buckwheat or brown rice noodles to make this gluten-free. It's best to prep all the vegetables first, as once you've cooked the noodles this is a fast dish cooked on a high heat in about 5 minutes!

15–20 MINS

4 nests of dried whole-wheat noodles (200g)

3 cloves of garlic

a thumb-size piece of fresh ginger

1 fresh red chilli

a bunch of scallions

1 red pepper

1 yellow pepper

1 carrot

150g shiitake mushrooms

1 head of pak choi/100g baby spinach

1½ tablespoons oil

For the dressing

1 x 400ml tin of coconut milk

juice of 1 lime

3 tablespoons tamari/soy sauce

1 tablespoon maple syrup

To garnish

a small bunch of fresh coriander or basil

3 tablespoons sesame seeds

pickled ginger (see page 149)

1 lime, cut into wedges

1. Put the noodles into a pot of boiling water with a pinch of salt and cook as per the instructions on the packet. Remove from the heat, drain, then rinse with cold water in a colander over the sink and set aside while you prepare your veg.

2. Peel and finely chop the garlic and ginger. Deseed and finely slice the chilli (leave the seeds in if you like it hot), and finely chop the scallions. Deseed and finely chop the peppers, and grate the carrot. Finely chop the mushrooms. Remove the nub at the end of the pak choi and finely chop the rest.

3. Put the oil into a non-stick large-bottomed pan (ideally a wok) on a high heat. Add the garlic, ginger and chilli, and cook for 1 minute, stirring regularly. Add the scallions, peppers, grated carrot and mushrooms and cook for a further 1½ minutes, stirring all the time.

4. In a cup, use a fork to mix together the dressing ingredients (don't worry if the coconut milk stays a bit lumpy – the mixture will break up once it's added to the pan). Add the dressing to the pan and stir right through so that it coats all the veg really well.

5. Next, throw in your noodles and heat for a minute. Add the pak choi or spinach and cook for another minute, until wilting.

6. Remove from the heat. Roughly chop the fresh coriander or basil and use to garnish each serving, together with sprinkles of sesame seeds. It's also nice with some kimchi, pickled ginger and wedges of lime.

SHIITAKE & SESAME STIR-FRY

This fast-cooking simple dinner is ready in a jiffy! The orange juice and tahini sauce is brilliant with the umami flavour coming from the tamari, and a lovely bang of ginger. Use buckwheat or brown rice noodles if you want to be gluten-free.

10 MINS

2 nests of dried whole-wheat noodles (100g)

For the sauce

3 cloves of garlic

a thumb-size piece of fresh ginger

2 tablespoons tahini

4 tablespoons tamari/soy sauce

200ml orange juice

For the stir-fry veg

150g shiitake mushrooms (or other mushrooms)

1 red pepper

1 large head of pak choi

a handful of sugarsnap peas

1 fresh red chilli

5 scallions

1 tablespoon oil

2 tablespoons sesame seeds

1. Boil a pan of water and cook the noodles as per the instructions on the back of the pack, then drain and rinse. Set aside in a colander over the sink.

2. For the sauce, peel the garlic and ginger, then put all the sauce ingredients into a blender and whiz till smooth (if you don't have a high-speed blender like a NutriBullet, chop the garlic and ginger before adding).

3. Chop your mushrooms, deseeded pepper, pak choi and sugarsnap peas into bite-size pieces. Finely slice half the red chilli and 4 of the 5 scallions, making sure to leave 1 scallion and half the chilli aside for garnish at the end.

4. Put a large saucepan on a high heat and add 1 tablespoon of oil. Add the scallions and fry for 1 minute, then add the rest of the veg and 3 tablespoons of your sauce and cook for 3–4 minutes.

5. Next, add the rest of the sauce and bring to the boil, stirring regularly. Once it boils, remove from the heat.

6. Serve the vegetable sauce on top of a bed of noodles. Finely slice the other half of the red chilli and the remaining scallion and use them to garnish, along with a sprinkling of sesame seeds.

GREEN CURRY NOODLE BOWL

We have taken a quick, easy Thai green curry and turned it into a super-tasty noodle bowl. Goes great any night of the week – sweet, savoury and substantial! Try to get wholewheat or buckwheat noodles, as they are much higher in fibre.

15 MINS

2 nests of dried whole-wheat noodles (100g)

2 cloves of garlic

a thumb-size piece of fresh ginger

1 fresh green chilli

1 red pepper

2 courgettes

a bunch of scallions

1½ tablespoons oil

½ teaspoon sea salt

1 x 400ml tin of coconut milk

3 tablespoons tamari/soy sauce

1 tablespoon maple syrup/other liquid sweetener

juice of 1 lime

2 teaspoons ground cumin

1 tablespoon ground coriander

a small bunch of fresh basil

To garnish

toasted sesame seeds

toasted cashew nuts/peanuts

chilli flakes

pickled ginger (see page 149)

kimchi (see pages 150-52)

1. Put a small pot of salted, boiling water on a high heat, add the noodle nests and cook as per the instructions on the back of the pack (we usually crunch the noodles in, as they are easier to eat when smaller). Drain and rinse in a colander, then set aside.

2. Peel and finely chop the garlic and ginger. Deseed and finely slice the chilli (leave the seeds in if you like it spicy). Deseed the red pepper and finely chop, along with the courgettes. Finely slice the scallions into small, thin pieces.

3. Put the oil into a wide-bottomed pan such as a wok over a high heat. Throw in the garlic, ginger and chilli and cook for 1½ minutes, stirring constantly.

4. Add the courgettes, scallions (reserving some for garnish), red pepper and salt and cook for a further 3 minutes, stirring regularly. Finally, add the coconut milk, tamari, maple syrup, lime juice, cumin and coriander, and cook for a further 3 minutes, until it boils. Remove from the heat.

5. Pick the basil leaves from the stalks, then finely chop the stalks and stir them through the curry. Put some noodles into the bottom of each bowl and top with the curry. Tear the basil leaves and sprinkle on top. Garnish with the toasted sesame seeds, toasted nuts, the reserved scallions, some beansprouts, chilli flakes, pickled ginger and kimchi. You can also add avocado, if you like.

SINGAPORE NOODLES

Despite its name, this dish is not common in Singapore, but is a standard Chinese dish. Instead of the usual vermicelli noodles, we use wholewheat ones – higher in fibre, yet equally tasty. Works well for lunch the next day too.

15 MINS

4 nests of dried wholewheat noodles (200g – use buckwheat noodles instead, for a gluten-free option)

a pinch of sea salt

1 x 300g block of tofu/tempeh, or 250g mushrooms

1 red pepper

1 yellow pepper

4 scallions

150g sugarsnap peas

2 cloves of garlic

1 thumb-size piece of fresh ginger

1 fresh red chilli

½ a carrot

2 tablespoons oil

3 tablespoons tamari/soy sauce

1 tablespoon curry powder

juice of 1½ limes

500ml vegetable stock

To garnish

a small bunch of fresh basil

sesame seeds

toasted cashews

chilli flakes

1. Put the noodles into a big pot of boiling water with a pinch of salt and cook as per the instructions on the pack. Drain, then rinse under cold water using a colander and leave them aside.

2. Cut the block of tofu into cubes, or chop the mushrooms. Finely slice the peppers and scallions, and chop the sugarsnaps in two. Peel and finely chop the garlic and ginger. Deseed and finely chop the chilli, and grate the carrot.

3. Put the oil into a large non-stick pan or wok on a high heat. Once the pan is hot, add the tofu or mushrooms together with the garlic, ginger and chilli. Stir continuously for 2–3 minutes, until the garlic and tofu or mushrooms start to turn slightly golden. Add the grated carrot and the tamari and cook for 2 minutes, stirring occasionally.

4. Next, add the scallions and peppers to the pan and cook for 2 minutes, stirring regularly. Add the curry powder and stir it right through for 30 seconds; if it starts to stick, squeeze the lime juice over at this point. Now add the cooked noodles, the vegetable stock and the lime juice (if you have not done above) and continue to stir. Allow it to cook for a further 2 minutes. Add the chopped sugarsnaps and stir them through just before removing from the heat.

5. Finely chop the basil and use it to garnish each serving. If you like, top with sesame seeds and cashew nuts and a sprinkle of chilli flakes.

TERIYAKI NOODLES

Here's our take on a teriyaki-style noodle dish – a tasty, quick dinner that's very flavoursome and really easy to make. We use wholewheat noodles, but you can use buckwheat or brown rice noodles for a gluten-free option.

15 MINS

4 nests of dried whole-wheat noodles (200g)

3 cloves of garlic

a thumb-size piece of fresh ginger

a handful of scallions

½ a fresh red chilli

150g oyster mushrooms

1 red pepper

1 head of pak choi

2 tablespoons oil

4 tablepoons tamari/soy sauce

1 tablespoon maple syrup

juice of 1½ limes

To garnish

chilli flakes

sesame seeds

toasted cashew nuts

fresh coriander

1. Bring a pot of water to the boil with a pinch of salt and cook the noodles in this as per the instructions on the packet, then drain and rinse in a colander. Set aside.

2. Peel and finely chop the garlic and ginger. Finely slice the scallions and chilli (remove the seeds if you don't like it spicy). Chop the mushrooms up nice and small, and finely chop the deseeded red pepper along with the pak choi.

3. Put the oil into a wok or large frying pan on a high heat. Once the pan is hot, add the garlic, ginger, chilli and scallions, and cook for 2 minutes, stirring regularly. Add the mushrooms and cook for another minute.

4. While these are cooking, prepare your sauce by mixing the tamari, maple syrup and lime juice together in a bowl. Add half the sauce to the pan, along with the red pepper and pak choi, and cook for 2 minutes.

5. Add the drained noodles to the pan along with the remaining sauce and cook for a further 2–3 minutes. Remove from the heat, divide between plates and top each serving with chilli flakes and sesame seeds, or maybe some toasted cashew nuts and chopped fresh coriander.

BLACK BEAN NOODLES & VEG

In a typical black bean sauce, fermented Chinese black beans are used, which can be hard to find. So instead, here we use tinned black beans and extra ginger and coconut milk to add a rich creamy base to this sauce. Makes a fab quick dinner or an excellent cold lunch for the next day. Great served with pickled ginger.

15 MINS

4 nests of dried wholewheat noodles (200g – use brown rice or buckwheat noodles for a gluten-free option)

For the sauce

1 x 400g tin of black beans

3 cloves of garlic

a thumb-size piece of fresh ginger

1 teaspoon vegetable stock powder/½ a vegetable stock cube

3 tablespoons tamari/soy sauce

1 tablespoon maple syrup

1 teaspoon white vinegar (ideally rice wine vinegar)

1 x 400ml tin of coconut milk

To cook

1 carrot

150g oyster mushrooms

1 red pepper

a handful of sugarsnap peas

1 scallion

1. Place the noodles in a pot of boiling water and cook as per the instructions on the pack. Set aside in a colander over the sink.

2. While the noodles are cooking, make the sauce. Drain the tin of black beans and rinse until there are no more 'suds'. Peel and roughly chop the garlic and ginger to make it easier on your blender. In a blender or food processor, whiz together all the ingredients for the sauce until well mixed.

3. Grate the carrot, then chop the mushrooms, the deseeded red pepper and the sugarsnap peas into small bite-size pieces. Finely slice the scallion and the chilli (removing the seeds if you like it milder).

4. Put a large wok or frying pan on a high heat and add the oil. Add the carrot, mushrooms, red pepper, sugarsnap peas, scallion, chilli and salt and cook for 2 minutes, stirring continuously. Next, add half your sauce and cook for a further minute.

5. Now drain and rinse the second tin of black beans and add to the wok/pan along with the noodles, the rest of the sauce and the lime juice. Cook for another 1–2 minutes, stirring all the time with a circular motion until the sauce is evenly distributed throughout the dish and everything is heated through.

1 fresh red chilli

1 tablespoon oil

½ teaspoon sea salt

1 x 400g tin of black beans

juice of ½ a lime/lemon

To garnish

chilli flakes

pickled ginger (see page 149)

6. Remove from the heat and garnish with chilli flakes and pickled ginger.

TOFU STEAKS WITH GINGER & SESAME

This is a dish our good friend Mark Lawlor always cooks. It packs some fab flavours – the ginger and tamari tastes carry wonderfully, and the sesame seeds and chilli add a lovely crunch that contrasts with the soft tofu. We love to serve these with some pan-fried or steamed broccoli, toasted sourdough, kimchi and wilted spinach. It's a super-tasty, nutritious and quick dinner! The oil can easily be left out to make it lower in fat, but it does give the tofu a lovely crisp crust.

10 MINS

2 cloves of garlic

a thumb-size piece of
   fresh ginger

½ a fresh red chilli

1 block of firm tofu (200g)

2 tablespoons oil

2 tablespoons sesame seeds

4 tablespoons tamari/
   soy sauce

100g baby/large leaf
   spinach

1. Peel and finely chop the garlic and ginger. Slice the chilli finely (removing the seeds if you want it milder). Chop the block of tofu along its side into four decent-sized rectangle-shaped tofu 'steaks' about 1cm thick.

2. Pour 1 tablespoon of oil into a pan (ideally a wide-bottomed non-stick one) and put on a high heat. Once the oil heats up, add the garlic, ginger and chilli and cook for 1–2 minutes, stirring regularly.

3. Transfer the garlic, ginger and chilli to a bowl and put the pan back on the heat. Add the remaining tablespoon of oil and the tofu steaks, ensuring that each one is fully touching the bottom of the pan. Sprinkle 1 tablespoon of sesame seeds over the steaks and add some of the garlic, ginger and chilli mix on top of each one. Leave the steaks to cook for 2–3 minutes, until they start to turn golden brown, then turn them over gently and sprinkle over the remaining sesame seeds as well as the rest of the garlic, ginger and chilli mix. Cook for another 2–3 minutes, until both sides are golden brown.

4. Now take the pan off the heat for a moment and add the tamari slowly, being sure to coat each steak (there will be a great big sizzle!). Put the pan back

on the heat and cook for almost another minute, turning the steaks in the tamari as it bubbles and the tofu absorbs the lovely flavours. Remove the tofu steaks and spoon the garlic, ginger and chilli from the pan on top of them.

5. Add the spinach to the same pan and leave it to wilt down for about 1 minute. Remove and serve alongside the steaks. Goes great with a nice slice of toasted sourdough bread (see page 162), steamed or pan-fried broccoli and some kimchi (see pages 150–52).

ULTIMATE FIFTEEN-MINUTE 'BURGER' ▶ / 'PULLED PORK' SANDWICH ▶ / VEGAN 'STEAK' ▶ /

'PHILLY CHEESE STEAK' / 'DONER KEBABS' ▶ / 'HOT DOGS' / 'SAUSAGE' ROLLS ▶ / 'MEATBALL' SUB ▶ /

BRUSSELS SPROUT CRISPS ▶ / CAULIFLOWER 'WINGS' ▶ / 'CHICK'N' NUGGETS ▶ / 'CHEESY' NACHO BOWL /

'MAC 'N' CHEESE' ▶ / 'TUNA' SALAD / SWEET CHILLI KETCHUP / VEGAN MAYONNAISE ▶ / COLESLAW ▶ /

'FETA' ▶ / 'MOZZARELLA' ▶ / 'NACHO CHEESE'

I CAN'T
BELIEVE
IT'S NOT...

ULTIMATE FIFTEEN-MINUTE 'BURGER'

Quick, easy to make, super-tasty, moreish - we are aware that's quite a promise, but these burgers will deliver! It's hard to get good-quality breadcrumbs, so we usually make our own by putting a few slices of decent bread into the food processor for a few minutes until they turn to crumbs. It is really worth seeking out the nutritional yeast, as it gives a nice distinct flavour, and a couple of slices of vegan cheese, while not essential, takes these burgers to the next level.

15 MINS

1 x 400g tin of kidney/
   black beans

1 red onion

2 cloves of garlic

150g oyster mushrooms (or
   any other mushrooms)

3 tablespoons oil

3 tablespoons tamari/soy
   sauce

100g breadcrumbs

2 tablespoons nutritional
   yeast

To serve

hummus/vegan mayo (see
   page 138)

sweet chilli ketchup/pesto
   (see pages 138 and 82)

a couple of slices of vegan
   cheese (optional)

lettuce leaves

tomato slices

red onion slices

ripe avocado slices

1. Drain and rinse the beans. Peel and finely chop the onion and garlic. Chop the mushrooms very finely.

2. Put 2 tablespoons of oil into a frying pan on a high heat. Once hot, add the onion and garlic and cook for 1–2 minutes, stirring regularly. Add the mushrooms and cook for a further minute. Now add the tamari, and fry for 2 minutes. Remove from the heat.

3. Put the breadcrumbs, beans and nutritional yeast into a bowl and mix well. Add the mushroom mixture to the same bowl and mix. Leave to cool for a minute, then use your hands or a wooden spoon to mash and mix everything together. Shape this mixture into 3 burger-shaped patties, making sure to really compress them so as to remove as much moisture as possible.

4. The patties are now ready to cook. We usually fry them in the pan in the remaining tablespoon of oil for 2 minutes on each side, until they go golden. You can also bake them in the oven at 180°C/350°F/Gas Mark 4 for 10 minutes, or throw them on the barbecue.

5. Serve in toasted burger buns with hummus/mayo on the bottom of the bun, sweet chilli ketchup/pesto on the top and any of the other topping options you fancy.

'PULLED PORK' SANDWICH

We first made this with our French friend Alex. We were very suspicious of it, but it turned out amazing – super-tasty and good enough to fool even the most carnivorous of your friends. You will need a tin of unripe green jackfruit, which is readily available in Asian stores or online.

20 MINS

For the pulled pork

1 x 400g tin of unripe green jackfruit

2 teaspoons ground smoked paprika

3 cloves of garlic, crushed

4 tablespoons tamari/soy sauce

2 tablespoons tomato purée

2 tablespoons cider vinegar

2 tablespoons neutral-tasting oil (e.g. sunflower oil)

4 tablespoons water

2 teaspoons maple syrup/agave syrup

To serve

4 burger buns/bread rolls

¼ portion of vegan coleslaw (see page 139)

a handful of fresh rocket leaves

1 ripe avocado (optional)

1. Preheat the oven to 200°C/400°F/Gas Mark 6.

2. Shred the jackfruit into thin little strips, pulling it apart with your hands and removing any seeds or tough ligament-type bits, as these can be too chewy. Transfer to a colander and rinse under cold water, then set aside.

3. Now make a barbecue sauce. Put the paprika, garlic, tamari, tomato purée, vinegar, oil, water and maple syrup into a medium-size bowl and mix well using a fork. Add the jackfruit, mixing very well with your hands to coat it all with the sauce. Spread the marinated jackfruit out well on a baking tray and bake in the preheated oven for 15 minutes, or until it smells amazing and is starting to brown and crisp up slightly.

4. Now assemble your sandwiches. Put a healthy serving of pulled pork into each burger bun or bread roll, along with a good couple of spoonfuls of coleslaw and some rocket leaves. Also goes great with slices of ripe avocado.

VEGAN 'STEAK'

'Vegan' and 'steak' are two words that do not typically go together, but bear with us! We were so pleasantly surprised the first time we tried this that we realized we were on to something. It has the same texture and consistency as steak without any of the negatives, and is a fraction of the price, both monetarily and environmentally. Worth trying. To make this, you do really need vital wheat gluten, which is available in many health food stores and online. This recipe makes 6–8 steaks, and we advise making it in full while you are going to the trouble - you can then use half your steaks to make our 'Philly cheese steak' (see page 119) or our 'doner kebabs' (see page 120).

40 MINS

For the steaks

½ x 400g tin of chickpeas

4 tablespoons nutritional yeast

1 teaspoon garlic powder

a good pinch of sea salt

2 tablespoons tamari/soy sauce

100g tomato purée

1 teaspoon smoked paprika

½ teaspoon freshly ground black pepper

100ml vegetable stock

1 tablespoon Dijon mustard

250g vital wheat gluten

1 tablespoon coconut oil

1. Drain and rinse the chickpeas and put them into a food processor. Add the nutritional yeast, garlic powder, salt, tamari, tomato purée, smoked paprika, black pepper, stock and mustard, and blend till smooth. Transfer this mixture to a mixing bowl, add the vital wheat gluten and mix it all very well - it should come together into a tight ball. Knead this with your hands for a couple of minutes to soften.

2. Now it is time to shape it into individual steaks. Cut the ball into about 6–8 smaller equal-size balls. Start shaping your balls into steaks by flattening them with the help of a potato masher or a meat tenderizer. Each steak should be about 2cm thick.

3. Set up a steamer over a pot of water and bring the water to the boil. In the meantime, cut as many pieces of tin foil as the number of steaks that you have, making sure each piece of foil is about double the length and width of each steak. Wrap each steak completely in the foil.

4. Place all the foil packages in the top section of the steamer, cover, and steam for about 20 minutes. Remove from the heat and allow to cool slightly before unwrapping. If making them ahead, you can now store your steaks in a sealed container in the fridge for 3-4 days.

*6 tablespoons tamari/
soy sauce*

1 teaspoon smoked paprika

1½ tablespoons maple syrup

5. To make the marinade, mix the tamari, smoked paprika and maple syrup together in a large, wide bowl. Soak the steaks in the marinade for a couple of minutes, turning them around really well so that they absorb as much of the marinade as possible.

6. Put 1 tablespoon of coconut oil into a non-stick pan on a high heat and cook each steak on both sides till it goldens up, starts to char and smells amazing! You will need to cook the steaks in batches, as you won't fit them all in the pan at one time.

7. Great served with salad or vegan coleslaw (see page 139).

Note: If there is not enough marinade for the amount of steaks you are making, simply make some more, using the same proportions!

'PHILLY CHEESE STEAK'

We lived in Philadelphia for a summer when we were twenty years old, teaching golf at a golf camp. We ate many a Philly cheese steak that summer (we ate everything back then!). This is our vegan version of the classic. It really gives the original a run for its money, without any of the animal fats or cholesterol. It's fun to make and will leave everyone looking for more!

15 MINS

2 vegan steaks (see page 116)

1 onion

100g mushrooms

2 tablespoons coconut oil/ other oil of choice

For the marinade

4 tablespoons tamari/soy sauce

1 teaspoon smoked paprika

½ teaspoon vinegar

1 tablespoon maple syrup

½ teaspoon garlic powder

To serve

2 hot dog buns/mini baguettes

vegan mayo (see page 138)

1 x nacho cheese (see page 141)

1. Put all the ingredients for the marinade into a bowl and mix well together with a fork. Cut the vegan steaks into strips and soak in the bowl of marinade for a couple of minutes, compressing the strips and encouraging them to absorb as much of the marinade as possible.

2. Peel and finely slice the onion, and cut the mushrooms into quarters. Heat the oil in a non-stick pan on a high heat and add the prepared onion and mushrooms. Cook for 2-3 minutes, stirring regularly, then move them to the side of the pan.

3. Now transfer the marinated steak strips to the other side of the pan and cook, stirring constantly, for 3-4 minutes or until they start to turn golden and slightly char - they will smell amazing! Remove from the heat.

4. Cut your buns or baguettes lengthways and spread some vegan mayo on the bottom of each one. Add some onion and mushrooms and divide the steak strips between the buns.

5. Top with a decent drizzle of nacho cheese, sandwich together and take a big bite!

'DONER KEBABS'

When we ate our first vegan doner kebab in Shoreditch, in London, we were totally inspired to create our own version. We make this using some leftover vegan steak (see page 116) and it works brilliantly. The lads in our kitchens (who know their way around a doner) said it tasted just like the Turkish original. To save time, you could simply buy some seitan to replace the vegan steak - it's readily available in most health food stores.

10–15 MINS

250g vegan steak (see page 116), or 250g seitan

1½ tablespoons coconut oil

For the marinade

4 tablespoons tamari/soy sauce

1 teaspoon smoked paprika

½ teaspoon vinegar

1 tablespoon maple syrup

½ teaspoon garlic powder

To serve

4 large pittas/wraps (ideally wholemeal)

vegan mayo (see page 138)

lettuce leaves (preferably cos or iceberg, but any green will work)

a few slices of tomato

kimchi (see pages 150-52)/sauerkraut/pickles

sweet chilli ketchup (see page 138)

1. In a bowl, mix together all the marinade ingredients using a fork. Finely slice the vegan steak or seitan so it is almost shredded. Add to the marinade, then press and mix it really well so that each piece gets a decent covering and soaks up all the flavour.

2. Put a shallow pan on a high heat and add the coconut oil. Once warm, add the marinated strips and cook for 3-4 minutes, or until they start to char a little, making sure to stir all the time so they cook evenly. Remove from the heat.

3. Toast the pittas in a toaster and slice them open along one side. Divide the strips into four portions. To assemble your pittas, start with some vegan mayo on the bottom, then some lettuce leaves, tomato slices and kimchi (or sauerkraut/pickles). Add your steak strips and top it off with a little drizzle of sweet chilli ketchup. You're in for a treat!

'HOT DOGS'

This is a good one – we got the chefs in our main kitchen to try them, and their verdict was that they were super-tasty and very close to the real deal. These freeze really well and keep for about 3 days in the fridge too. Simply heat up in a pan for 2 minutes each side (defrosting them first, if frozen), until golden.

65 MINS

1 medium onion

4 cloves of garlic

1 tablespoon oil, plus extra for frying

150g tinned butter beans

150ml vegetable stock/water

2½ tablespoons tamari/soy sauce

50g tomato purée

2 teaspoons smoked paprika

1 teaspoon ground coriander

1 teaspoon ground cumin

1 teaspoon Dijon mustard/ wholegrain mustard

½ teaspoon freshly ground black pepper

½ teaspoon sea salt

125g vital wheat gluten (see page 116)

30g porridge oats

2 tablespoons nutritional yeast

1 tablespoon ground flax seeds/ground chia seeds

1. Peel and finely chop the onion and garlic. Put the oil into a small pan on a high heat, then add the onion and garlic and cook for 2 minutes, stirring regularly. Transfer the onion mixture to a food processor.

2. Drain and rinse the beans and add to the processor along with the vegetable stock, tamari, tomato purée, smoked paprika, coriander, cumin, mustard, black pepper and salt. Blend until smooth.

3. Put the vital wheat gluten into a large mixing bowl along with the oats, nutritional yeast and ground flax seeds, and mix well. Add the contents of the food processor to the bowl and stir until combined. If it seems too dry to come together, add another tablespoon or two of vegetable stock. Knead by hand in the bowl for about 2 minutes, until it all combines into a lovely well-formed ball.

4. Set up a steamer over a pot of water and bring the water to the boil.

5. In the meantime, cut 6–8 pieces of tin foil or baking parchment, each about double the length and width of a regular hot dog. Divide the mixture into 6 or 8 equal pieces. Place a piece of foil or parchment on the counter. Roll a piece of hot dog mix between the palms of your hands until it's about the size and shape of a hot dog. Place it on the foil or paper and roll it up, pressing lightly with your hands, to give it an even shape, then fold or twist the ends closed. Repeat with the remaining mix to form 6–8 vegan hot dogs!

To serve

6-8 small baguettes or hot
   dog rolls

vegan mayo (see page 138)

sweet chilli ketchup
   (see page 138)

mustard

kimchi (see pages 150-52)

6. Place all the hot dogs in the top of the steamer,
   cover, and steam for about 40 minutes. Remove
   from the heat and allow to cool slightly before
   unwrapping. If you want to keep your hot dogs to eat
   at a later time, store them in a covered container in
   the fridge for up to 3 days.

7. To cook, simply put 2 tablespoons of oil into a non-
   stick frying pan on a high heat, place your hot dogs
   in the pan and cook, turning them constantly, till they
   golden up and start to smell delicious.

8. Serve in a baguette or hot dog roll, with some vegan
   mayo, sweet chilli ketchup, mustard and kimchi (or
   any other type of pickles).

'SAUSAGE' ROLLS

As young lads growing up, we ate lots of sausage rolls at every party in our house and have very fond memories of them. Recently we came up with a plant-based version, which to our surprise tastes very similar to those of our childhood memories!

30 MINS

1 x 340g pack of ready-rolled puff pastry

oil, for brushing the pastry

2 tablespoons white or black sesame seeds

For the sausagemeat filling

1 x 400g tin of butter beans

3 cloves of garlic

100g walnuts

2 tablespoons tamari/soy sauce

4 tablespoons ground flax seeds

1 teaspoon sea salt

½ teaspoon smoked paprika

1 teaspoon ground coriander

½ teaspoon freshly ground black pepper

2 tablespoons oil

1 tablespoon dried Italian herbs (e.g. rosemary or oregano)

To serve

sweet chilli ketchup (see page 138)

1. If your pastry is frozen, defrost it – this is best done by removing it from the freezer the night before and putting it into the fridge overnight.

2. Preheat the oven to 200°C/400°F/Gas Mark 6 and line a baking tray with baking parchment.

3. To make the filling, drain and rinse the butter beans and put them into a food processor with the rest of the filling ingredients. Blend until smooth.

4. Place the sheet of puff pastry on the baking parchment and cut it in half lengthways. Take little bits of the filling mix and, using your hands, roll them into mini sausages about 2½cm in diameter. Place them lengthways in the middle of the halved puff pastry, with the long side of the sausages parallel to the long side of the puff pastry. Add more sausages until they cover the full length of the puff pastry. Roll up the pastry, starting from the longer side, so that it fully covers the sausages, ensuring that the two ends of the pastry meet. If there is any excess pastry, simply roll it under so that the seam is underneath, then seal with water or oil.

5. With a pastry brush, brush the length of the pastry with oil and sprinkle with sesame seeds. Then cut the roll into small bite-size pieces, about 4cm long. Repeat these steps with the second half of the puff pastry, then spread the sausage rolls out evenly on the baking sheet.

6. Bake in the preheated oven for 20 minutes, until the sausage rolls turn lovely and golden. Leave to cool, then enjoy with some sweet chilli ketchup.

'MEATBALL' SUB

These non-meat meatballs are really 'meaty', if you know what we mean! This is a quick dinner/lunch that's very satisfying. Ensure you use the sun-dried tomatoes that are the dried fruit type ones rather than the ones in oil. They should be readily available.

20 MINS

30g sun-dried tomatoes

1 tablespoon ground flax seeds

3 tablespoons water

1 small red onion

2 cloves of garlic

150g oyster mushrooms (or any mushrooms)

1 x 400g tin of kidney beans

2½ tablespoons oil

3 tablespoons tamari/soy sauce

100g breadcrumbs

2 tablespoons nutritional yeast

For the tomato sauce

1 x 400g tin of chopped tomatoes

1 teaspoon maple syrup/ other liquid sweetener

a pinch of sea salt

2 tablespoons sun-dried tomato pesto (optional)

1. Soak the sun-dried tomatoes in boiling water for 5 minutes before using. Make a flax egg by mixing the ground flax seeds and water together in a bowl and leaving it to sit for a few minutes.

2. In the meantime, peel and finely chop the onion and garlic. Finely chop the mushrooms. Drain the kidney beans and rinse thoroughly.

3. Heat 1½ tablespoons of oil in a medium-size pan on a high heat. Add the onions and garlic and fry for 1 minute, stirring regularly. Then add the mushrooms and the tamari and cook for 2 minutes, until the mushrooms are nice and brown. Remove from the heat and transfer the mixture into a large bowl.

4. To make your tomato sauce, get a new saucepan and put in the chopped tomatoes, maple syrup and salt. Place over a medium heat and let it simmer away while you make the meatballs, stirring occasionally.

5. Drain and finely chop the soaked sun-dried tomatoes – the easiest way to do this is using scissors. Add them to the bowl of mushroom mixture, together with the kidney beans, breadcrumbs, nutritional yeast and flax egg. Mix well, then form into golf-ball-size balls with clean hands.

3 small or medium baguettes/some slices of good-quality bread

a handful of rocket

1 ripe avocado

6. Pour 1 tablespoon of oil into a medium-size non-stick frying pan and fry the meatballs in batches on a high heat for about 2 minutes each side, until they start to get golden. Be careful not to crowd the pan or they might not get crispy.

7. While the meatballs are frying, finish off your tomato sauce by adding the sun-dried tomato pesto (if using) and mixing well.

8. To serve, spread the tomato sauce on your baguettes or bread, add 3 or 4 meatballs to each sub, and garnish with a little rocket and some sliced avocado.

BRUSSELS SPROUT CRISPS

We stumbled upon this wonder when peeling Brussels sprouts – we didn't want to waste what we were peeling off, so we decided to bake them and see if we could make crisps. They turned out fab and we ended up serving them as a part of our Christmas dinner! They work great as an appetizer with drinks, too.

20 MINS

30 Brussels sprouts

3 tablespoons oil

a good pinch of sea salt

chilli flakes

1. Preheat the oven to 180°C/350°F/Gas Mark 4.

2. Peel the jackets off the Brussels sprouts and fill a baking tray with them. Cover well with the oil, salt and chilli flakes. Mix well, ensuring that each jacket has a little coating of oil, salt and chilli.

3. Bake in the preheated oven for 20 minutes, or until the sprouts start to go golden and crisp.

CAULIFLOWER 'WINGS'

Not a chicken in sight! This might sound crazy as an idea, but these 'wings' work out fab – great as a snack and as finger food.

25 MINS

1 head of cauliflower

1 tablespoon tomato purée

4 tablespoons oil

2 tablespoons tamari/soy sauce

1 tablespoon apple cider vinegar

1 teaspoon smoked paprika

1 teaspoon garlic powder

¼ teaspoon chilli powder

1 tablespoon maple syrup/ other liquid sweetener

2 tablespoons water

1. Preheat the oven to 200°C/400°F/Gas Mark 6. Chop the cauliflower into wing-size pieces and put into a bowl.

2. Put the rest of the ingredients into a bowl and whisk together, using a fork, until a nice smooth mixture forms.

3. Pour this marinade over the cauliflower and mix to coat thoroughly. Transfer the marinated 'wings' to a baking tray and bake in the preheated oven for 20 minutes, or until they are nice and crispy.

4. Great served with our vegan mayo (see page 138), sweet chilli ketchup (see page 138) or vegan nacho cheese (see page 141).

'CHICK'N' NUGGETS

We came up with more than ten different versions of these one afternoon, trying to get the right texture and bite while keeping the recipe easy and quick to make. We reckon we got it right with this recipe – let us know what you think!

25 MINS

For the nuggets

100g cashew nuts

50g oat flakes

6–10 tablespoons water

30g vital wheat gluten
  (see page 116)

½ teaspoon garlic powder

½ teaspoon onion powder

½ teaspoon sea salt

2 tablespoons sunflower oil

a pinch of freshly ground
  black pepper

For the coating

100g breadcrumbs

¼ teaspoon ground turmeric

non-dairy milk, to help coat
  with the breadcrumbs

For frying

2 tablespoons sunflower oil

1. Soak the cashew nuts in boiling water, leave to sit for 10 minutes, then drain.

2. Put your oat flakes into a blender and blend for 30 seconds till they form a flour-like powder. Transfer the blended oat flakes to a food processor and add all the remaining nugget ingredients, starting with the water and remembering to include the drained cashew nuts. Whiz until it all starts to come together into a dough (about 30 seconds). If you think it needs more moisture, add an extra couple of tablespoons of water.

3. Remove the dough from the blender, bring it all together with your hands and start forming it into small nugget shapes.

4. In a bowl, mix the breadcrumbs and turmeric for the coating. Put some milk into a second bowl and dip the nuggets in this before rolling each one in the coating, making sure they are well covered.

5. Put a wide-bottomed non-stick pan on a high heat. Once warm, pour in 2 tablespoons of oil and add the nuggets in batches that will fit your pan without crowding it. Cook for a couple of minutes on each side, until they are golden and starting to brown. Alternatively, you can bake them in a preheated oven on a baking tray at 180°C/350°F/ Gas Mark 4 for 10 minutes on each side.

6. These are great served with hummus, sweet chilli ketchup (see page 138) or kimchi (see pages 150–52) on the side. You could also stuff them inside a toasted pitta with hummus and slices of tomato, some vegan mayo (see page 138) and kimchi. Yum!

'CHEESY' NACHO BOWL

A healthier take on the original here, as we bake the tortillas instead of deep-frying them. Combined with a lovely zingy salsa and refried black beans, it makes a fab shared snack for parties - defo one of our favourite sharing party plates! This is based on a Mexican dish called chilaquiles, which we had a variation of in our friend Luca's fab café, the Fumbally. If you're in a rush, simply replace the tortillas with your favourite tortilla chips to save time!

20 MINS

6 wholewheat tortilla wraps

vegetable oil

sea salt

For the refried beans

1 x 400g tin of black beans

2 cloves of garlic

a small bunch of fresh coriander

1 tablespoon oil

1 tablespoon ground cumin

1 teaspoon ground coriander

2 tablespoons tamari/soy sauce

juice of 1 lime

For the salsa

2 cloves of garlic

2 scallions

1 x 400g tin of chopped tomatoes

100g tomato purée

juice of ½ a lime

1 tablespoon ground cumin

1. Preheat the oven to 200°C/400°F/Gas Mark 6.

2. Brush both sides of each tortilla with a light layer of vegetable oil and cut into 8 wedges (or other shapes as desired). Place the tortilla pieces in a single layer on a baking tray (you may need two trays), sprinkle with salt and bake in the preheated oven until lightly browned, about 8–10 minutes.

3. In the meantime, start making the refried beans. Drain the black beans and rinse thoroughly. Peel and finely chop the garlic. Finely chop the coriander leaves. Put the oil into a frying pan on a high heat, add the garlic and fry until it starts to turn golden, then add the beans, cumin, coriander, tamari and lime juice. Using the back of a wooden spoon, start mashing the beans, while continuing to fry for 2 minutes, adding a little water to prevent the beans from sticking to the pan. Add half the chopped fresh coriander leaves, mix through and remove from the heat.

4. Once the tortillas have browned, remove from the oven and leave to cool.

5. Now make your salsa. Peel and roughly chop the garlic, finely slice the scallions and put them both into a food processor with the rest of the salsa ingredients. Blend until smooth and set aside.

1 teaspoon maple syrup/
other liquid sweetener

1 teaspoon sea salt

½ teaspoon chilli powder

To serve

1 red onion

1 ripe avocado

1 red chilli

200g nacho cheese
(see page 141), or
cheese of choice

a small bunch of fresh
coriander

2 tablespoons black
sesame seeds

6. Peel the red onion and chop into thin half-moon-shaped slices. Remove the avocado from its skin and chop into small bite-size pieces. Cut the chilli into thin strips – if you want it milder, remove the seeds first.

7. Now assemble your nacho bowl. Tip the crispy tortilla shapes in first, then pour over the refried beans. Now add the fun stuff – the nacho cheese, avocado, onions and salsa (if you want the tortillas to remain crunchy, serve the salsa on the side). Chop the fresh coriander finely and sprinkle on top with some black sesame seeds and the sliced red chilli. You can also serve this in individual bowls if it's not a sharing plate. Make sure everyone gets all the toppings!

'MAC 'N' CHEESE'

We first made this with our lovely Canadian friend Rose, from the Cheap Lazy Vegan YouTube channel. We had never eaten mac 'n' cheese before! We've adapted the original recipe to make it creamier and we think even better!

15 MINS

175g raw cashew nuts

1 x 500g pack of wholewheat macaroni or penne

2 cloves of garlic

juice of ¾ of a lemon

½ teaspoon ground turmeric

2 tablespoons nutritional yeast

1 tablespoon smooth mustard, such as Dijon

¼ teaspoon chilli powder

1 teaspoon sea salt

125ml unsweetened almond milk or oat milk

100ml neutral-tasting oil (e.g. sunflower or mild olive oil)

50ml water

To garnish (optional)

nutritional yeast

chilli flakes

fresh thyme leaves

1. Boil a full kettle and pour a quarter of the water into a small pot. Add the cashew nuts and bring to the boil, then reduce to a simmer for 10 minutes, until the cashews are soft.

2. Pour the rest of the boiling water into a medium-size pot and cook the pasta with a pinch of salt as per the packet instructions.

3. In the meantime, peel the garlic and whiz in a blender with the remaining ingredients. When the cashews are ready, drain and add them to the blender too, whizzing again until nice and creamy.

4. Once the pasta is cooked, drain it, then return it to the pot or put it into a warmed serving bowl and mix the sauce through.

5. Serve topped with some additional nutritional yeast and some chilli flakes and thyme leaves if you have them.

'TUNA' SALAD

We were getting a tin of jackfruit ready to make a faux pulled pork sandwich (see page 114) when we realized that the jackfruit looked just like tuna, so we came up with this recipe on the back of that! This super-simple recipe works great as a sandwich filler and will keep for about a week in a sealed container in the fridge.

5–10 MINS

1 x 400g tin of unripe green jackfruit

1 red onion

2 cloves of garlic

3 scallions

150ml vegan mayonnaise (see page 138)

sea salt

a pinch of freshly ground black pepper

5 small gherkins (optional)

1. Drain the jackfruit and rinse off all the brine in a colander. Using your hands, break the jackfruit apart into a bowl, removing any very fibrous bits that would be too chewy.

2. Peel and finely slice the onion and garlic, and finely chop the scallions. Add these to the jackfruit along with the vegan mayonnaise, salt and black pepper. Mix well, using a spoon.

3. If using, chop up the gherkins and mix them through to give your salad some crunch and zing.

4. Enjoy in a toasted sandwich, with fresh leaves, tomato and a little avocado.

SWEET CHILLI KETCHUP

Quick, super-easy to make and takes a basic ketchup to the next level! For a basic spice-free ketchup, just leave out the chilli.

200g tomato purée | 120ml maple syrup | 5 tablespoons apple cider vinegar/white wine vinegar | 5 tablespoons water | 1 teaspoon sea salt | ½ teaspoon chilli powder | a pinch of freshly ground black pepper

1. Mix all the ingredients in a bowl, using a fork, until it is smooth and well mixed. Add more or less chilli to suit your taste buds. Enjoy as a dip or with your burger!

VEGAN MAYONNAISE

This recipe is just so good. Although it was in our last book, we include it here too, as we use it in a good few recipes in this book. It is a super-tasty mayo that is just like the real thing, easy to make and goes splendidly with just about everything! These are some of the recipes where we use it:

Coleslaw (see this page), Philly cheese steak (see page 119), Doner kebabs (see page 120), Egg mayo (see page 60)

2 cloves of garlic | 300ml soya milk | 2 tablespoons lemon juice | ½ teaspoon sea salt | ¼ teaspoon freshly ground black pepper | 1 tablespoon Dijon mustard | 300ml olive oil

1. Preheat the oven to 180°C/350°F/Gas Mark 4. Wrap the garlic cloves in foil and roast them for 10 minutes, until soft.

2. Squeeze the garlic out of its skin and put into a blender along with all the rest of the ingredients except the olive oil. Blend for 1 minute, then slowly pour in the olive oil with the blender running until the mixture emulsifies to a mayonnaise-like texture.

3. Keeps for up to 10 days in the fridge, in a sealed container.

COLESLAW

Growing up, we used to love nothing more than a coleslaw sambo. Having not had one in years, we decided to come up with our own vegan version – quick, tasty and delicious – which makes a wonderful sandwich filler or basis for a salad! You'll only need half a portion of vegan mayonnaise for this recipe.

vegan mayonnaise (see page 138) | 250g red cabbage | 250g white cabbage | 75g carrot | ½ a white onion

1. First make the vegan mayo.

2. For the coleslaw, finely grate the red cabbage, white cabbage and carrot (a food processor works fine for this). Peel and finely chop the onion and mix all the veg together in a large bowl. Add half the mayonnaise (the other half will keep for 10 days in a sealed container in the fridge). Coleslaw ready to go!

3. We love to serve this in a toasted sandwich, with pan-fried oyster mushrooms and wilted spinach with cherry tomatoes (see page 40).

'FETA'

This is a really good plant-based alternative to feta. It works great cubed into salad, crumbled on top of pizzas or in a sandwich.

145g ground almonds | 40ml lemon juice | 120ml water | 3 tablespoons sunflower oil/ other neutral-tasting oil | 2 cloves of garlic, finely chopped | 1¼ teaspoons sea salt

1. Preheat the oven to 140°C/275°F/Gas Mark 1 and line a baking tray or loaf tin with baking parchment.

2. Put all the ingredients into a blender and whiz together until you get a lovely, smooth and uniform mixture. Depending on your blender, you may have to stop blending and scrape down the sides a few times, as the mixture is quite dry.

3. Get a clean J-cloth or cheesecloth and spoon the mixture into the middle of it. Bring all the edges of the cloth together to tightly wrap the mixture. Squeeze gently for a minute or two to eliminate any excess moisture.

4. Transfer the cheese mixture to the prepared baking tray or loaf tin. Spread it out so that it is 2cm thick, then put into the preheated oven and bake for 30 minutes.

5. Remove and leave to cool. Store in the fridge for up to a week, in an airtight container.

'MOZZARELLA'

This one started out as a wild goose chase and we weren't at all sure if it would work out, but it ended up being a winner and very similar to the real thing. It's also quick and easy to make – you just need to soak the nuts the night before.

100g cashew nuts, soaked overnight | *200ml water* | *1 tablespoon nutritional yeast* | *1½ teaspoons apple cider vinegar* | *1 teaspoon sea salt* | *¼ teaspoon garlic powder* | *3 tablespoons tapioca flour*

To serve

2 slices of sourdough toast | *1 clove of garlic* | *a little rapeseed oil* | *a handful of cherry tomatoes* | *a handful of fresh basil leaves*

1. If you did not have time to soak the cashew nuts overnight, just boil them for 10 minutes to soften them. Put the drained cashew nuts and the water into a blender and blend until smooth.

2. Now add the nutritional yeast, apple cider vinegar, salt, garlic powder and tapioca flour to the blender and whiz again until smooth. It should be the consistency of pancake batter.

3. Put this mixture into a non-stick saucepan over a high heat and stir continuously until it starts to thicken. Be patient, this may take 5–10 minutes or so. When the mixture comes together into one ball, transfer it to a bowl. With wet fingers (to prevent sticking), grab small bits of the mixture and form them into golf-ball-size mozzarella-type balls.

4. If not using immediately, transfer to a jar of brine (made by mixing 400ml of water with about 2 teaspoons of salt). The mozzarella will keep like this in the fridge for up to a week.

5. Use as you would use regular mozzarella. We put ours on sourdough toast, rubbed with garlic, with a drizzle of oil, some chopped cherry tomatoes and fresh basil leaves – it really hits the spot!

'NACHO CHEESE'

This is a runny yet thick full-flavoured 'cheese' that will make your nachos, tacos, burritos, burgers, hot dogs, sandwiches and even baked potatoes into a mouth-watering feast!

60g carrots | 80g potatoes | 560ml sunflower oil | 30ml rice milk | 1 tablespoon lemon juice | 1½ teaspoons arrowroot flour/ tapioca starch | 1 teaspoon garlic powder | 1 tablespoon nutritional yeast | ¾ teaspoon sea salt | a pinch of freshly ground black pepper

1. Roughly chop the washed carrots and potatoes to the same size and put into a medium saucepan over a high heat. Cover with water, bring to the boil and cook until soft.

2. Put the cooked potatoes and carrots into a blender with the rest of the ingredients and whiz until smooth.

3. Keeps in the fridge for up to a week. Serve with corn chips, tacos or nachos to destroy those cheesy cravings!

FERMENTASTIC!

THE BASICS OF PICKLING

Pickling and fermentation is one of Steve's favourite hobbies – he always has lots of different experiments on the go. Pickling is the process of preserving food by anaerobic fermentation, which means the bacteria do not require air to ferment and create lactic acid. In order to achieve this, food is generally submerged under water. People have pickled foods for centuries. It's a super-healthy, cheap and delicious way to enjoy the taste of fresh food throughout the year. Also there's something wonderful about checking on how your foods develop to find the perfect recipe and process!

There are two main methods of pickling:

1. Vinegar brine method

2. Natural fermentation method

Although both of these methods work, we generally use the natural fermentation process, as we want to develop good gut bacteria for better digestion and overall health. When using vinegar, as in the pickled red onions recipe (see page 148), the vinegar kills the good bacteria (commonly referred to as probiotic bacteria) necessary for fermentation, as well as the bad bacteria.

In the natural fermentation process, food is not sterilized but creates a safe environment in which healthy lactic acid bacteria can develop and thrive. Lactic acid bacteria are naturally present on everything that grows, and by creating the right selective environment for these bacteria, you allow them to feed on the sugars that are also naturally present in vegetables. Through this process, the probiotic bacteria – which are so good for everything from digestion to immunity – grow and breed!

THE RIGHT ENVIRONMENT
FOR FERMENTATION PICKLING

There are three key elements you need to create a healthy environment for fermentation pickling:

1. **Temperature:** Room temperature is the ideal temperature for pickling. About 20°C is an optimal temp at which to ferment, but in our experience a wide range of 'room' temperatures work, and there are microclimates within any given house or apartment. If things are starting too slow in the winter, we move them closer to the hot press or warmer spots. Warmer temperatures will speed up fermentation but may make it happen too quickly, leading to a faster decomposition of your tasty ferment and, sometimes, a less crisp pickle. Lower temperatures will slow it down, or even prevent it.

2. **Submersion:** There are different kinds of fermentation. Some require air, others require no air. Pickles are the airless, or anaerobic, type, so when pickling, your veggies must be completely submerged under water. There are many ways to do this – the more basic approach is to use a plate or saucer to weight down the vegetables in the jar or pot. Look online for lots of interesting ideas about how to make your own cheap pickling pot.

3. **Salt:** This is not essential for fermentation, but it is better to make pickles with salt than without it for a few reasons:

- It helps to strengthen the pectins present in the vegetables, giving you a crisper pickle.

- Lactic acid bacteria (the type of bacteria you want) are relatively salt-tolerant, whereas some of the less desirable bacteria aren't.

- Salt will slow fermentation and make your ferment last longer.

HOW LONG TO FERMENT FOR?

Fermentation time will vary according to your acidity preference, but a good rule of thumb is 1-2 weeks in the summer and 2 weeks in the winter. There are some pickles that take longer.

Storage time will vary depending on the vegetable fermented, the amount of salt used and the temperature at which it is stored. We generally try to eat our pickles before 3 months have elapsed, but we have in some cases eaten pickles that were still delicious after 6 months or even a year. One of our favourite things about fermented foods is that, for the most part, they let you rely on your senses. If it looks slimy, feels too soft or smells or tastes 'off', it is time for the compost pile.

Follow a recipe or some general guidelines the first time you ferment something. Fermentation creates strong smells and flavours, and if you are not used to this, you might think the 'right' smells are actually wrong.

QUICK PICKLING
TROUBLESHOOTING

o **Surface mould** – oh no! You didn't submerge your veggies enough, or maybe some bits floated to the surface. Best to discard and start a new batch, ensuring you submerge more vigilantly.

o **The brine is cloudy** – this is a good thing! Fermented brine gets cloudy because it is loaded with good stuff, like lactic acid bacteria. Cloudy means it has worked. When you are done with your pickles, drink that stuff or add it to cold soups for probiotic punch, or to bread dough for flavour and salt.

PICKLED GARLIC

When you pickle garlic, the fermentation process makes it soft, tender and not as pungent as raw garlic. It also brings it to another level of healthiness, as it produces loads of probiotic bacteria, which are great for our microbiome and gut flora. Peel garlic in less than 10 seconds by banging the whole head with the heel of your hand or using a large knife to separate the cloves. Get two large bowls – put all the garlic into one, put the other bowl on the top so they are like a sphere, and shake like crazy for 10 seconds – easy peasy peeled garlic!

Here we use plenty of salt, as we don't envisage you chomping on this pickle, but rather using it as a seasoning and flavour carrier. Use organic garlic if you can.

10 MINS PREP

250ml filtered/tap water at room temperature

1 tablespoon sea salt

4 heads of garlic, cloves peeled and separated (try the method above)

1. Pour the water and salt into a clean sterilized jar 500ml or larger and stir until the salt dissolves. Put your peeled garlic cloves into the jar.

2. Make sure the garlic is kept away from air – you may need to use a small plate, a smaller jar, or some other heavy weight to hold it down below the surface of the water to ensure it ferments properly.

3. Let your jar sit at room temperature for at least 4 weeks, away from direct sunlight. You may want to check at the 2-week point to make sure the brine (salt water) hasn't evaporated. If the brine is low, add a touch more.

4. The garlic is getting close to done when the smell of it changes from harsh, raw garlic to the alluring aroma of roasted garlic. Now it's ready to get stuck into and enjoy.

5. Adding pickled garlic to your hummus and pesto recipes makes them insanely tasty!

PICKLED RED ONIONS

We use these bright pink piquant beauties a lot in the café. They don't require much effort to make and are so worth trying! You can use them for so many things – to add more flavour to a sandwich, to garnish dishes or to add to salads. Technically these are better pickled using a vinegar brine method, in order to get the wonderful pink colour. Be sure to store your pickled onions in a glass or ceramic container – most metals will react with the vinegar, and plastic will absorb the flavours.

5 MINS PREP

3-4 medium red onions, approx. 500g

½ tablespoon sea salt

550ml rice vinegar/white wine vinegar/apple cider vinegar

1. Peel the onions and slice into thin rings.

2. Dissolve the salt in the vinegar in the clean sterilized jar or container that you will be using to store the onions. Add the onions to the jar and stir gently to spread the flavours. The vinegar should cover the onions, but if not, add a little water to fill the jar to ensure the onions are completely submerged.

3. Cover the jar with a lid or a clean tea towel, and leave the onions on the countertop out of direct sunlight for a few hours (but preferably a few days). Then store in the fridge. They will keep for several weeks, but are best within the first week.

PICKLED GINGER

Also known as gari in the sushi world, this is a wonderful condiment to add to noodle dishes, stir-fries, sandwiches and curries. It's super-easy to make and keeps for months in the fridge. Store-bought pickled ginger often contains additives, preservatives and colouring agents to make the ginger pink, but ours is additive-free – we use beetroot juice to give that lovely pink hue! This uses the vinegar brine method (see page 144) and is super-easy to make at home.

5 MINS PREP

½ a small fresh beetroot

150g fresh ginger

150ml rice vinegar/vinegar of choice (as long as it's clear)

½ teaspoon sea salt

30ml agave syrup

1. Start by making some beetroot juice to colour the ginger. It's best to wear gloves for this, as it can get messy. Grate the beetroot (no need to peel), then squeeze the grated beetroot over a bowl to get the juice. Discard the squeezed beetroot, as you won't need this again.

2. Peel the ginger, slice finely into thin strips and put into a clean sterilized jar about 500ml in size.

3. Mix the vinegar, salt and agave syrup in a small pot over a low heat until the salt dissolves and everything is well mixed. Pour this liquid over the sliced ginger and leave to cool.

4. Next, add the beetroot juice, stir and put the lid on. Leave the ginger to ferment on the countertop out of direct sunlight for about a week, then store in the fridge for up to 3 months.

TRADITIONAL KOREAN KIMCHI

This kimchi has a more full, crunchy mouth-feel and more spice compared to our basic recipe on page 152. We have left out the fish sauce and prawns – normally used – and replaced them with tamari and a little kelp powder. The exotic-sounding gochugaru is simply Korean chilli powder made without the seeds – you'll get it in most Asian shops. Replace it with chilli powder and paprika if you can't get it. This recipe is for 1.5kg, but it's well worth doubling – it's a wonderful healthy condiment to have on hand or to give as a gift.

120 MINS PREP

1kg Chinese leaf cabbage/ napa cabbage (approx. 1 large cabbage), or pak choi

60g sea salt

160ml water

25g rice flour/plain flour

1 teaspoon maple syrup/ other sweetener of choice

1 medium carrot

3 scallions

100g daikon radish (if you do not have this, replace with extra carrot or leave out)

½ a small white onion (20g)

6 cloves of garlic (20g)

½ a thumb-size piece of fresh ginger

60ml tamari/soy sauce

½ teaspoon kelp powder (optional)

10g gochugaru, or 5g chilli powder and 10g sweet paprika

1. Chop the cabbage or pak choi into thin, bite-size pieces. Put into a large bowl of water, rinse to remove any sand or soil, then drain.

2. Add the salt to the bowl and mix well, rubbing the salt around each leaf with your hands. If this seems like a massive amount of salt, don't worry, it will be washed off later! Leave for 30 minutes, then mix again and leave to sit for another 30 minutes. Mix one more time and again wait 30 minutes. This triple mixing will soften the cabbage, give it a salty flavour and kill off any potentially harmful bacteria.

3. While the cabbage is being prepared, make the rice porridge. Put the water into a pot and sift in the flour. Bring to the boil on a medium heat and stir for about 3 minutes, until the mixture starts to thicken. Add the maple syrup or sweetener of choice. Once it has thickened, but before it has reached the consistency of thick porridge, remove from the heat and transfer to a bowl to cool.

4. Meanwhile, grate the carrot, chop the scallions finely and chop the daikon radish into matchstick shapes.

5. Now make your chilli paste. Peel the onion, garlic and ginger and put into a blender along with the tamari and kelp powder, if using. Whiz until smooth. Add the gochugaru, or chilli powder and paprika, and mix well. Add this paste to the sweet rice porridge and mix well.

6. Gently squeeze out any remaining water from the cabbage. Rinse and drain three times to remove the surface salt. Return it to the bowl and add the carrot, scallions, radish, and the chilli paste. Stir the chilli paste mixture in really well so that each piece of Chinese cabbage is well coated with it.

7. Decant to a sterilized container/jar of choice (ideally a 2 litre jar) and push down so that the brine covers all the veggies. Leave a little bit of space at the top of your jar or container, as the brine normally rises and can overflow.

8. Put a lid on and leave at room temperature to ferment for 3-5 days, out of direct sunlight. After that, store in the fridge and allow the flavours to develop.

EASY KIMCHI

Definitely one of our favourite condiments, kimchi is like a Korean-style sauerkraut with a spicy, tangy, gingery flavour. This recipe was developed by Fiona, our wonderful fermenter, through lots of experimenting. 4kg might seem a lot, but it's worth making in bulk as it keeps, often gets better with age and makes a great present.

20 MINS

1kg white cabbage

1kg red cabbage

1kg fresh beetroot

1kg carrots

4 litres water

5 tablespoons sea salt

3 fresh red chillies

7 cloves of garlic

a bunch of scallions

75g fresh ginger

1. Grate the cabbage, beetroot and carrots (no need to peel) roughly (a food processor works fine) and place in a large bowl (big enough to take the 4 litres of water).

2. Now make a brine: put the water into a big pot and add the salt, mixing well. Pour this over the grated veg, making sure everything is completely submerged. Leave to soak for 12 hours or overnight.

3. Drain the veg but don't rinse them, reserving a small amount of the salty water for later. Roughly chop the chillies, garlic and scallions. Peel the ginger and grate finely. Add all these to the bowl of grated veg and mix through thoroughly.

4. Fill a clean glass jar with the mixture, making sure to compact it tightly. When you press down on the veg, some liquid should rise to the surface. If your mix is too dry, add some of the reserved salty water. It is this salty liquid that preserves everything and allows fermentation to happen – without it, everything will rot.

5. Place a clean plate, a smaller jar, or some other heavy weight on top of the mix to keep it compressed under the water. Seal with an airtight lid and leave for at least 2 weeks to ferment.

6. Check the kimchi every few days, making sure the veg stay submerged. Sometimes the top layer that's exposed to the air can start to go off slightly. It can simply be scraped off. The layer underneath will be fine to eat. Your kimchi can be left to ferment for up to a month.

ELENA'S FIG, LEMON & GINGER WATER KEFIR

Steve brews kefir all the time at home and his kids love it! It's a fermented drink that's high in probiotic bacteria, which are good for your gut, digestion and immune system. You will need water-based kefir grains for this, but don't be put off – all the info you need is on page 155. The beauty of kefir is that it only takes 3 or 4 days to brew, is easy to flavour and makes a great healthy alternative to sugary drinks. Brewing it at home is like having a pet, but a really nourishing pet. This recipe comes from our acro-yoga friend Elena. She gave Steve his first kefir grains, which he now cherishes and loves dearly.

15 MINS PREP

a thumb-size piece of fresh ginger

1 dried fig

2 slices of unwaxed lemon

1 litre spring/distilled water (drinkable tap water will do)

4 tablespoons water kefir grains

60g white cane sugar

1. Chop the ginger into small chunks and rip the dried fig in half. Place in a large sterilized jar with the rest of the ingredients and stir a little, then cover with a clean muslin cloth, which allows air to enter. Leave to ferment at room temperature (ideally 20°C), out of direct sunlight, for 2-3 days.

2. Once fermented, simply drain in a plastic sieve (never use metal, as it can kill the kefir grains). Remove the fig, ginger and lemon and discard, but save all the grains for the next batch. You will notice there are now more grains, as they have fed off the sugar and have grown, so you can now increase production or share with a friend. Decant into a sterilized glass litre bottle.

3. The water kefir is now ready to drink, but you can adjust the flavour by adding different flavoured tea bags, such as mixed berry, to this solution and leaving it to brew for an hour or so. You could add a little apple juice to make it a little sweeter. There are so many different combinations to flavour it – we suggest you get the basics down and then have fun, experimenting with flavours.

4. To brew more, just follow the steps above. If you want to increase the amount you make, use the same ratio.

KEFIR Q&A

Q: What are kefir grains?

A: Although they look a bit like grains (hence the name), they are actually mini bacteria and yeast existing in a symbiotic relationship.

Q: How much sugar is in kefir?

A: Like kombucha and milk kefir, water kefir's final sugar content is dependent on how long you allow it to ferment. As it ferments, the grains consume the sugars and convert them to carbon dioxide, acids, bacteria and yeasts. The final product after fermentation should contain the same amount of sugar as one green apple.

Q: Is there alcohol in kefir?

A: It is true that alcohol is a by-product of fermentation, and this applies to water kefir. Because water kefir does not contain as much acetic acid as kombucha (see page 156), its flavour does not have as much of a tangy punch. So any alcohol present is slightly more noticeable in water kefir, but the amount in the final ferment is so little, it is practically non-existent.

Q: Where can I get water kefir grains and can I make them from scratch?

A: Unfortunately, the answer to the latter is no. You will have to get them online (which is reasonably cheap and easy), or else from a friend who brews their own and has spare grains.

KOMBUCHA

Kombucha is a wonderful fermented tea that is rich in probiotics and good bacteria for your gut and immune system. It is a great alternative to fizzy drinks, as it naturally carbonates. Traditionally kombucha is made using black tea, but Fiona, our wonderful fermenter, makes two main varieties in the shop: a mixed berry kombucha, based on rooibos tea (caffeine-free), and a lemongrass and ginger kombucha, based on green tea. There is something rewarding about fermenting your own kombucha at home and growing a good 'mother' (or SCOBY - symbiotic culture of bacteria and yeast), which converts the sugar to probiotic bacteria. See the Q&A on pages 158-9 for all the info you'll need on sugar, SCOBY and fermentation time.

15 MINS PREP

1 litre spring/distilled water (drinkable tap water will do)

2 tea bags of your choice

60g white cane sugar (see page 159)

1 SCOBY (can be bought online, or follow our steps on pages 158-9 to make your own)

180g previously brewed or purchased kombucha

1. Pour 200ml of the water into an empty kettle and boil. Once boiled, add your tea bags along with the sugar and stir until the sugar has dissolved and the tea bags have really given their flavour (about 5 minutes). Remove the tea bags and discard.

2. Pour the remaining 800ml of water into a 1 litre sterilized glass jar and pour in the brewed sugary tea. Leave this liquid to cool until it is below 37°C (body temperature). If it is hotter, it will kill the SCOBY.

3. Add your SCOBY and the previously brewed or purchased kombucha to the jar. Cover with a clean tea towel and leave to sit for 10-15 days, out of direct sunlight, at room temperature.

4. After this time, remove your SCOBY and it is ready to go! This is your FIRST fermentation. If you would like to make your kombucha more carbonated and add different flavours, you can do a SECOND fermentation as follows.

5. Divide your kombucha between several smaller jars/bottles, adding a pinch of sugar to each. Put different tea bags, such as mixed berry or lemongrass and ginger, into each jar, to play with the flavour a bit more. Put a lid on each jar.

6. After you have let the kombucha sit in the smaller, sealed jars/bottles for a day, you will need to 'burp' it. This means that you take the lid off to let it expel some gas, then put the lid back on straight away.

7. Leave it to sit for 1–3 more days, then it will be ready to drink! The longer you leave it, the more it will carbonate/bubble.

KOMBUCHA Q&A

Q: How long should I ferment kombucha?

A: If your SCOBY is healthy and the room temperature is about 20°C, it should take about 10-14 days. However, if it's hotter it will take less time; if it's colder it will take more time. Also, if your SCOBY is small it will take longer. When your kombucha is ready it should be naturally bubbly and not too sweet (this indicates that the SCOBY has consumed the sugar and converted it to probiotic bacteria and carbon dioxide/bubbles). So taste the kombucha, and once it is to your liking and bubbly, it is good to go! The longer you ferment your kombucha, the more acidic or vinegar-like it becomes.

Q: What should I use to ferment my kombucha in?

A: Ideally use a glass jar, but plastic (ideally BPA-free) also works fine. Avoid using metal containers and cutlery, as it can damage the SCOBY.

Q: Where can I get a SCOBY?

A: You can buy them online cheaply and easily. A better way is to get one from a friend who brews their own kombucha: each time you brew a batch, the SCOBY grows and can be divided and shared with friends to brew their own kombucha.

Q: How do I grow a SCOBY from scratch myself?

A: This is easy but takes a little more time. Get a 500ml store-bought bottle of raw kombucha. Boil the kettle and brew a small cup of tea with 2 tablespoons of sugar (ensuring you use the same tea type used in the store-bought kombucha – normally black, green or rooibos). Leave to cool to below 37°C.

Pour the kombucha into a larger jar or glass bottle and add the cup of sweet tea, which will give the yeast and bacteria additional food to consume during the process of growing a new culture. Cover with a dry clean muslin cloth so that the air can still get at it. Keep at room temperature and out of direct sunlight for 2-4 weeks. After a week, it is common to see a baby SCOBY developing across the top of the liquid – it starts off as a blob of clear film, then slowly becomes whiter and thicker as time goes on. If there are no signs of a SCOBY appearing after 3 weeks, discard the batch and start again. You need the SCOBY to be at least ½cm thick before using it to brew your first batch of kombucha tea. Reaching that thickness may take up to 30 days. Keep the kombucha tea and the new SCOBY for making your first batch of kombucha and follow the instructions in the recipe on page 156.

Q: I thought sugary drinks were bad? I never consume sugar, so it puts me off kombucha.

A: The sugar in kombucha is not for you, it's for the SCOBY to consume. When fermented, there will be 2–6g of sugar per 236ml glass of unflavoured kombucha. By contrast, the same size glass of orange juice has about 24g of sugar. If fermented longer, say for 3 weeks or more, the sugar levels in kombucha may be even lower.

Q: Why does kombucha need so much sugar?

A: Without sugar, kombucha cannot ferment. Sucrose is most easy to digest by the yeasts; they consume the sugar and put out carbon dioxide (bubbles) and ethanol.

Q: What type of sugar should I use to brew kombucha?

A: There are many different views here, but it's pretty straightforward. Most sugars are fine for kombucha, but you'll see there are a few provisos:

Plain white sugar – the kombucha consumes this easiest.

Brown sugar – this is harder for the kombucha to break down and will also change the flavour significantly. Experiment first and see if you like it.

Honey – a wonderful choice, but avoid using unheated honey, as the bacteria will disturb the kombucha/SCOBY balance and could brew up a dangerous concoction.

Agave syrup – this can turn the brew sour, so best to combine it with another sugar type that contains glucose for the long-term health of the culture.

SOURDOUGH BREAD

Sourdough bread is bread that is fermented and uses natural yeast in the air to raise it. It has an elegance about it that much modern bread misses, in that it requires simply flour, water and salt to make. Sourdough bread has something magical and mystical about it. Steve watched the Michael Pollan documentary *Cooked* (the episode called 'Air'), and decided to grow his own sourdough mother in order to really understand the process. After simply mixing flour and water, it started to bubble and sour, and after a few days he had a sourdough mother – a new pet that needed feeding and love! This was the birth of Steve's love and fascination with sourdough bread. It's very easy to get started and Steve really cannot say enough positive things about the beauty of making fresh bread in your own home and having another mother to love and look after! He highly recommends you give it a go.

MAKING YOUR OWN SOURDOUGH MOTHER FROM SCRATCH:

10 MINS

100g flour (we prefer 100% wholewheat or wholemeal spelt)

100ml water

1. Put the ingredients into a 400ml clean jam jar and mix until well combined. Cover with a tea towel, to keep out flies but still allow air and natural yeast to enter. Leave on the worktop for 3-5 days, out of direct sunlight.

2. Once it smells yeasty and slightly beery or brewery-like, and has small bubbles in it, it is ready for its first feed. You now have your very own sourdough mother, which will hopefully nourish you and your friends and family!

3. A point to note is that whatever flour your mother culture was created with is the flour you will always have to feed it, so for example if you used wholemeal spelt flour, your mother culture will need to be always fed wholemeal spelt flour.

FEEDING YOUR NEW MOTHER CULTURE:

Your sourdough culture will now need to be fed daily. If you are going on holiday, either get a friend to feed it or simply put it in the fridge, where it will live for a week without feeding.

Pour half your mother culture into a bowl – this will be used to make bread. Now, to the same jar, add:

50g flour (the same flour used for your mother culture)

50ml water

Mix well and set aside.

CROWD-PLEASING HEALTHY SOURDOUGH LOAF

Normally Steve bakes 100% wholemeal bread to maximize nutrition and fibre, but on occasion he breaks out and uses some white flour to give a more indulgent loaf. This recipe is a total crowd-pleaser. It's made with 50% wholemeal, 50% white flour but looks brown when baked. It does take a little time to perfect it, but it is so well worth making your own sourdough loaf at home!

You will ideally need a proving basket; if you don't have one, a well-floured bowl will do fine.

30 MINS

300ml sourdough mother culture (see page 160)

250g wholemeal flour

250g strong white bread flour

200ml water

a generous pinch of sea salt

1. In a large bowl, mix all the ingredients really well, then tip on to a lightly floured surface and knead for 5–10 minutes, until super-elastic. To test whether the dough is ready, stretch it out to about 70cm long – it should come back to the original size.

2. Lightly coat the dough with a dusting of flour, put it into a clean bowl, cover with a tea towel and leave to rise for 2 hours in a warm place. After 2 hours the dough should have nearly doubled in size. Time to shape it for its final ferment.

3. Lightly flour your work surface or tabletop. Stretch out the dough to about 70cm long, then fold it back on itself three times (nearly like rolling it). This process develops more structure for the bread to rise and gives an air pocket in the bread.

4. On one side of the folded dough, create a seam by pressing down with the base of your palm to seal one end. Now roll the dough towards yourself as tightly as possible. Flour your proving basket (or bowl) to prevent the dough from sticking, then coat the dough in flour and gently place in the basket or bowl. Let it rise for 8–12 hours, again in a warm place.

5. After this time, the dough should have nearly doubled in size. Preheat the oven to 240°C/475°F/Gas Mark 9 and coat a baking tray with a drizzle of oil and a dusting of flour. Gently tip the dough on to the baking tray, making sure you don't knock any of the air out. If you want to be very professional, use a razor blade to give your bread a quick signature cut on the top. Often bakers do this to encourage the bread to open in a certain direction and to give it their own signature.

6. Put your bread into the preheated oven and at the same time put a roasting tray with some water in it in the bottom of the oven to create some steam, which will give your bread a good crust. Bake for 30 minutes, until it's well browned and makes a hollow sound when you tap the base.

WORTH THE WAIT MAINS

SHEPHERDLESS PIE

Our take on a classic comforting family dinner, this pie is easy to make and goes down a treat on a cold winter's night. Perfect with a simple dressed green salad.

50 MINS

For the lentil mixture

2 red onions

4 cloves of garlic

½ a medium carrot

½ a medium parsnip

100g fine green beans

2 x 400g tins of cooked lentils

2 tablespoons oil

1 teaspoon sea salt

2 x 400g tins of chopped tomatoes

½ teaspoon freshly ground black pepper

1 teaspoon smoked paprika

2 bay leaves

1 tablespoon maple syrup

2 tablespoons tamari/soy sauce

a few sprigs of fresh flat-leaf parsley

For the mashed potato topping

1kg potatoes

3 tablespoons olive oil

100ml non-dairy milk

sea salt and freshly ground black pepper

1. Peel and finely chop the onions and garlic, and finely slice the carrot and parsnip. Cut the fine beans into bite-size pieces. Drain the lentils and rinse thoroughly. Put the oil into a large pan on a high heat, add the onions and garlic and cook for 2 minutes, stirring regularly. Add the carrot and parsnip together with the salt, and cook for 3 minutes, stirring regularly.

2. Add the drained lentils to the pan, along with the chopped tomatoes, black pepper, smoked paprika, bay leaves, maple syrup and tamari. Bring to the boil, then lower the heat and add the fine beans and parsley (roughly chopped) for some colour. Leave to simmer, checking from time to time that the mixture is not sticking to the pan. Continue to simmer while the potatoes cook, stirring occasionally to ensure nothing sticks to the pan.

3. Preheat your oven to 200°C/400°F/Gas Mark 6.

4. While the filling is simmering, chop the potatoes evenly into small bite-size pieces and put them into a medium pot. Cover with boiling water, bring back to the boil, then reduce the heat and leave to simmer until tender (about 15 minutes). Drain the potatoes, return them to the pot and mash with a potato masher, adding the oil and non-dairy milk a little at a time until your mash reaches the right texture (smooth but not sloppy). Taste and season with salt and pepper.

5. Tip the lentil mixture into a lasagne-type casserole dish and top with the mashed potato (aim for approximately half lentil and half potato). Bake in the preheated oven for 20–30 minutes, until the top of the potato is turning golden and starting to crisp. Remove from the oven and serve.

HEARTY GREEK STEW

This is one of those recipes that you crave when you come home on a cold evening - comforting, easy and full of goodness. Tomato sauces in Greece have cinnamon and allspice, quite foreign to Irish or Italian tastes, but actually go wonderfully when given time to cook and mellow. Fabulous served with big hunks of bread to soak up the juices.

25 MINS

2 medium red onions

3 cloves of garlic

1 small carrot

1 head of fennel

1 courgette

500g potatoes, unpeeled

250g fine green beans

2 tablespoons olive oil

500ml vegetable stock

2 x 400g tins of chopped tomatoes

1 tablespoon maple syrup/ other liquid sweetener

1 teaspoon ground cinnamon/1 cinnamon stick

½ teaspoon allspice

1 teaspoon dried oregano

1 bay leaf

1½ teaspoons sea salt

½ teaspoon freshly ground black pepper

½ a lemon

To garnish

a handful of fresh flat-leaf parsley

1. Peel the onions and garlic and chop finely. Grate the carrot and finely chop the fennel. Cut the courgette and potatoes into small bite-size pieces. Top and tail the green beans.

2. Pour the oil into a large frying pan over a high heat. When it heats up, add the garlic and onions, stirring regularly until the garlic turns golden and the onions start to go translucent, about 5 minutes.

3. Add the carrot, fennel, courgettes and potatoes, and cook for a further 3 minutes on a high heat.

4. Next, add the vegetable stock, chopped tomatoes, maple syrup, cinnamon, allspice, oregano, bay leaf, salt and black pepper. Once it boils, reduce the heat, put a lid on and leave to simmer for 15 minutes, stirring occasionally.

5. Check the potatoes after 15 minutes to see if they are soft and ready to eat, then add the green beans. Quarter the lemon, removing any obvious seeds, add to the dish and cook for a further 5 minutes with the lid off.

6. Garnish each serving with flat-leaf parsley. This dish goes great served with crusty hunks of bread and some Kalamata olives on the side.

HEARTY HUNGARIAN GOULASH

A simple, elegant and humble dinner that will warm the cockles of your heart! Lovely served with brown rice or quinoa and a few decent hunks of good-quality bread.

30 MINS

1 large onion

3 cloves of garlic

1 carrot

1 red pepper

1 yellow pepper

1 courgette

3 potatoes, unpeeled

200g mushrooms
(2 good handfuls)

2 teaspoons oil

sea salt

1 x 400g tin of pinto beans/
borlotti beans/butter
beans

1 x 400g tin of chopped
tomatoes

800ml vegetable stock

3 tablespoons tomato purée

2 tablespoons tamari/soy
sauce

1 tablespoon ground cumin

1 teaspoon ground
cinnamon

½ teaspoon smoked paprika

½ teaspoon freshly ground
black pepper

1 bay leaf

1. Peel and finely chop the onion and garlic. Finely slice the carrot, deseeded peppers, courgette and potatoes. Chop the mushrooms into quarters.

2. Heat the oil in a large pot on a high heat. Add the chopped onion and garlic and cook for 2 minutes, stirring regularly. Add the carrot and a pinch of salt and cook for 2 minutes. Now add the peppers, courgette, potatoes and mushrooms and cook for a further 2 minutes, stirring regularly.

3. Next, drain and rinse the beans and add along with all the remaining ingredients. Bring to the boil, then reduce to a simmer for 10 minutes, stirring occasionally.

4. Taste if the carrot and potatoes are cooked – if so, your dinner is ready! Season with more salt and pepper if you think it needs it.

ONE-POT LASAGNE

This is literally a one-pot lasagne that doesn't even need to go into the oven! We cook the lasagne by soaking the sheets in boiling water while making the tomato sauce, then top everything off with a super-tasty cashew cheese. We think this is epic, super-original and a real breakthrough! Well worth making.

60 MINS

250g lasagne sheets (½ a pack)

2 tablespoons oil (for brushing the lasagne sheets)

For the cashew cream

250g raw cashew nuts

150ml vegetable stock

50ml olive or sunflower oil

1½ tablespoons apple cider vinegar/lime juice

3 tablespoons nutritional yeast (optional)

a pinch of sea salt and freshly ground black pepper

½ teaspoon onion powder (optional)

½ teaspoon garlic powder (optional)

For the tomato sauce

1 onion

3 cloves of garlic

200g mushrooms

1 courgette

1. First soak the cashew nuts for the cashew cream in 300ml of boiling water for 30 minutes.

2. Boil a full kettle and pour the boiling water into a large bowl. Using a pastry brush, brush both sides of each lasagne sheet with oil so they are properly coated. Put them into the water (oiling them will stop them sticking together while they are part-cooking in the water).

3. For the tomato sauce, peel and finely chop the onion and garlic, finely slice the mushrooms and slice the courgette into thin half-wheels. Chop the chilli finely, removing the seeds if you prefer less heat. Lastly, chop the sun-dried tomatoes very finely (easiest if you use scissors).

4. Get a wide ovenproof pot (no plastic/wooden handle and ideally a similar height/depth to a casserole dish) and put on a high heat. Add 2 tablespoons of oil to the pan and leave to heat up. Add the onion, garlic and chilli, and fry for 2 minutes, stirring regularly, until the garlic is turning golden and the onions are going transparent. Now add the mushrooms and courgette and continue to fry for about 3 minutes, stirring regularly.

5. Next, add the red wine and allow to reduce for 2 minutes. Pour in the chopped tomatoes together with the tomato purée, sun-dried tomatoes, maple syrup, salt and black pepper. Bring to the boil, then reduce the heat and simmer for 10 minutes. Turn off the heat.

6. While your tomato sauce is simmering, make your cashew cream. Drain and rinse the soaked

½ a red chilli (if you like
  it spicy)

5 sun-dried tomatoes

2 tablespoons oil

100ml red wine

2 x 400g tins of chopped
  tomatoes

100g tomato purée

1 tablespoon maple syrup

½ teaspoon sea salt

¼ teaspoon freshly ground
  black pepper

cashews. Put all the ingredients for the cashew cream into a blender and blend until really smooth.

7. Time to layer up your lasagne. Remove half the tomato sauce and put aside, leaving the other half in the pot to use as a base. Remove the lasagne sheets from the bowl of water and separate them if they have stuck together a little. Use half of them to form a layer on top of the base tomato sauce, cutting the sheets with scissors so that they properly fit the pot (don't overlap them).

8. On top of your first layer of lasagne sheets, pour half the cashew cream and spread it evenly across the edges. Next, add the remaining tomato sauce and spread it out evenly. Top with another layer of lasagne sheets as before, then finish by spooning the remaining cashew cheese on top and spreading it smoothly and evenly.

9. Once layered up, put a lid on the pot and cook on the hob on a medium to low heat for 5-10 minutes. If you have time and have a grill, remove the lid and place the lasagne under the grill for another 5-10 minutes until it starts to turn golden.

10. Having served lasagne for years in our café, we find it surprising how few people know that the easiest and best way to cut lasagne is with scissors. So cut it with scissors, serve and enjoy!

PIZZA THREE WAYS

How to make pizza that 'tastes great and a little healthier' was the motivation for this one. There are lots of ways to make the base, and here we're giving you a no-yeast recipe that is super-quick. To be gluten-free, try buckwheat flour instead. The tomato sauce is full of flavour, to balance the dense wholemeal base. Our topping suggestions are pretty out there, but they are delicious and really work!

30 MINS

For the base:

200g white flour

200g wholemeal flour, plus extra for dusting

2 teaspoons baking powder

¾ teaspoon fine sea salt

2 tablespoons oil

220ml water

For the tomato sauce:
(makes 500 g)

8 sun-dried tomatoes

2 cloves of garlic

1 x 400g tin of chopped tomatoes

2 tablespoons olive oil

1 tablespoon maple syrup

½ teaspoon sea salt

a pinch of freshly ground black pepper

1½ teaspoons balsamic vinegar

1. Preheat the oven to its maximum temperature.

2. Sift the flours and baking powder into a bowl, then add the salt and oil. Mix well in a circular motion, using your clean hands held in a claw-like shape.

3. Make a well in the middle and slowly add the water. Coat your hand with a little flour and mix until all has come together. Divide the dough into four equal-size balls.

4. Coat a rolling pin with a little flour to stop it sticking. No need to knead the dough, just roll it out using the rolling pin. Roll each ball out as thin as you can (no more than 5mm thick), to ensure a crispy thin base.

5. Sprinkle a little oil and flour on a baking tray to prevent sticking, then gently place your base on the tray and bake in the preheated oven for 8 minutes, without any topping, to ensure a crispy base.

6. Meanwhile, in a small pot, boil the sun-dried tomatoes for 5 minutes, until they become soft and easier to blend, then drain. Peel the garlic.

7. Put all the ingredients for the tomato sauce (including the sun-dried tomatoes) into a blender, and whiz until smooth.

continued on next page »

TOPPINGS

Here are three of our favourite topping suggestions (each recipe is enough for four pizzas).

POTATO, RADICCHIO, CHEESE & WALNUTS

30 MINS

1kg waxy potatoes (such as Ditta or Maris Piper)

2 tablespoons oat milk

3 tablespoons olive oil

¾ teaspoon sea salt

1 teaspoon ground ginger

1 head of radicchio

100g vegan cheese, or other cheese of choice

25g walnuts

1. Boil the potatoes until soft, drain, then mash using a potato masher or large fork, adding the oat milk, olive oil, salt and ground ginger until the mash is thick but has a nice creamy taste.

2. Chop the radicchio in half, remove the firm core in the centre and bottom that is holding it together, and cut the rest into thin, small bite-size pieces. Grate the cheese. Lightly crush the walnuts.

3. Slather a generous serving of tomato sauce on your precooked pizza base, but aim for only a quarter of the sauce you've made – you don't want to make the base soggy. Gently spread over the mashed potato to give a decent base layer. Next, sprinkle on about three-quarters of the radicchio, the lightly crushed walnuts and a good handful of cheese.

4. Transfer to a warmed baking tray and bake in your hot oven for 8 minutes, until the base is nice and crispy and the topping is turning golden. Bake for longer if the base is still soft. Sprinkle with the rest of the radicchio to give it a nice pop of colour.

KALE, MUSHROOM, CHEESE & ALMONDS

30 MINS

100g kale

2 tablespoons olive oil

a pinch of sea salt

100g vegan cheese, or other cheese of choice

100g oyster mushrooms, or other mushrooms of choice

3 tablespoons tamari/soy sauce

30g flaked almonds

1. Using your clean hands, remove the kale from its stalks and rip into bite-size pieces. Add the oil and salt and massage for a minute, allowing the salt to tenderize the kale.

2. Grate the cheese. Roughly chop the mushrooms and put them into a bowl. Add the tamari and mix well so that each piece of mushroom gets nicely coated.

3. On your pre-cooked pizza base, spread a generous serving of tomato sauce (about a quarter of the quantity you've made). Cover with kale, a good sprinkling of cheese and some oyster mushrooms, and sprinkle some almonds on top.

4. Lay the base on a heated baking tray and put into the hot oven for 4–6 minutes, until the cheese melts and the base starts to brown slightly.

FIG, ASPARAGUS, CHEESE & CASHEW NUTS

30 MINS

4 fresh figs

100g vegan cheese, or other cheese of choice

200g fresh asparagus, or trimmed fine green beans

1 tablespoon oil

a pinch of sea salt

25g cashew nuts

1. Thinly slice the figs and grate the cheese. If using asparagus, remove the woody base of each spear. In a bowl, dress the asparagus spears with the oil and salt.

2. Spread about a quarter of the tomato sauce you've made on your pre-cooked pizza base, then sprinkle over the cheese and a layer of figs. Top with asparagus and a sprinkle of whole or chopped cashew nuts.

3. Transfer to a warmed baking sheet and cook in the hot oven, until the cheese melts and the base starts to brown slightly and crisp.

RAINBOW SUSHI BURRITOS

We had our first vegan sushi burrito from a food truck at the Big Feastival in the Cotswolds, in the UK – delish! This is our version of the fast-growing food trend. It's great for party finger food or lunch on the go. You'll need 5 nori sheets and a bamboo rolling mat to assemble these – available from Asian supermarkets.

60 MINS

5 sheets of nori seaweed

For the rice

500g short-grain brown rice/ white sushi rice

1 litre water

1 teaspoon ground turmeric

For the veg fillings

½ a ripe mango

½ a ripe avocado

½ a carrot

¼ of a red cabbage

½ a red pepper

For the sweet chilli shiitake filling

100g shiitake mushrooms

4 tablespoons oil

2 tablespoons tomato purée

2 tablespoons maple syrup

¼ teaspoon sea salt

½ teaspoon chilli powder

1. First step is to cook the rice. Get two medium-size pots, and add 250g of rice and 500ml of water to each pot. Add the turmeric to one of the pots (the turmeric will turn this batch of rice yellow). Put both pots on a high heat and bring to the boil. If using short-grain brown rice, stir regularly – this will encourage it to release its starch and make it stickier. Once the water boils, reduce both pots to a simmer, with the lids on. Once the water has nearly all evaporated, remove from the heat and set aside with the lids on to sit for 5 minutes, to puff right up.

2. While your rice is cooking, prepare the fillings. For the mango, peel, slice the flesh off the stone and finely slice it into batons. For the avocado, remove the stone, remove the flesh from the skin and slice into fine strips. Finely slice the carrot into thin matchstick-type batons and finely slice the red cabbage. Lastly, remove the seeds from the red pepper and slice into fine long strips.

3. To make the sweet chilli filling, finely chop the shiitake mushrooms and set aside. Mix the rest of the ingredients together in a bowl, using a fork, then add the mushrooms and mix well. Put a pan on a high heat and, once it is hot, cook the mixture for 2–3 minutes, stirring regularly.

4. Once the rice is cooked, spread each colour out on a baking tray to cool, keeping them separate. In a mug or bowl, mix the ingredients for the rice sauce together using a fork. Pour this over the cooled rice, spreading it between the trays and mixing it well through.

For the rice sauce

7 tablespoons rice wine
  vinegar

2½ tablespoons agave syrup
  (or other, preferably clear,
  liquid sweetener)

a pinch of sea salt

To serve

tamari/soy sauce

wasabi

pickled ginger (see page 149)

kimchi (see pages 150-52)

5. Prepare a small bowl of water to seal your burrito
    sushi rolls after rolling. Take a nori sheet and place
    on top of a bamboo rolling mat, with the smooth
    side underneath and the rough side on the inside.
    Spread the rice, whichever colour (usually works best
    with one colour per roll), on top of the nori sheet in a
    nice thin layer about 1cm thick, leaving a 2½cm gap
    at the top of the sheet (for ease of rolling). Spread
    right up to the bottom edge as well as both sides
    of the sheet. Starting from the bottom edge of the
    rice, widthways, layer on a shallow strip of each of
    the veg in 'rainbow' rows, so they are tightly packed
    and almost overlapping, with a strip of the chilli
    shiitake filling alongside. Lift the bamboo mat with
    your thumbs and, while applying pressure to the veg,
    slowly roll the nori sheet around till it meets the other
    end, working hard to keep it nice and tight. One part
    of the nori sheet should overlap the nori sheet from
    the other end. Dip your finger in water and run it
    along the sheet, 'sealing' it together like you would
    an envelope. That's one burrito done!

6. Repeat the process with the remaining nori sheets,
    rice and veg, mixing and matching the veg in
    different colours until everything is used up.

7. Serve with small shallow dipping dishes of tamari,
    wasabi, pickled ginger and kimchi.

FEVZIYE'S TURKISH LEEK DISH

If you have not yet discovered the delicate taste of leeks, here is a simple, easy and healthy recipe for you. This is a dish that we first ate in Turkey when our brother Darragh's mother-in-law, Fevziye, cooked it for us. In Mediterranean style, a big amount of good-quality extra virgin olive oil is used for braising the leeks with carrots and rice in this dish. Cooking the vegetables slowly without much stirring gives this dish its unique flavour, and it tastes even better the next day. Serve it either as a light main dish when warm, with some wholemeal bread, or as a cold side dish the next day.

30–40 MINS

1 medium onion

2 large carrots

500g leeks

4 tablespoons extra virgin olive oil

2 tablespoons basmati rice or bulgur

1 tablespoon sweetener (maple syrup/agave syrup)

1½ teaspoons sea salt

a pinch of freshly ground black pepper

225ml hot water

juice of ½ a lemon

To serve

fresh flat-leaf parsley or dill leaves (optional)

lemon wedges

1. Peel the onion and slice finely. Slice the carrots into half-moons. Cut the leeks into 5cm diagonal slices, including the green bits.

2. Place a large, wide, heavy-based saucepan on a high heat with 2 tablespoons of the oil. Once the oil is hot, add the onions and carrots and sauté for 2 minutes, or until the onions get translucent.

3. Add the leeks and cook for about another 5 minutes, or until the leeks start to soften, stirring gently and making sure they don't burn. Add a couple of tablespoons of water if they start to stick.

4. Next, add the rice, sweetener, salt and pepper, then drizzle the hot water and lemon juice over (we were told that the lemon juice helps to make the veg shinier when cooking).

5. Reduce the heat, cover the pan with a lid and let the leeks and carrots simmer slowly over a low heat for about 20 minutes, or until the water is almost gone and the vegetables are tender. Avoid stirring during this stage, to prevent the starch from the rice coming out and damaging the vegetables. If all the water is absorbed before the veg are ready, add a little more to stop them burning.

6. When the leeks and the rice are cooked, take the dish off the heat and leave it to cool down with the lid on. Put a clean tea towel or paper towel between the pan and the lid, if there seems to be excess moisture.

7. If you are going to serve this as a cold side dish, leave it to cool down to room temperature, then remove the lid, pour the remaining olive oil evenly over the vegetables and move them around in the pan to get the oil through, again trying not to stir. If you would rather not use this much oil, you can skip this step.

8. When you are ready to serve, ideally slide the mixture into a serving bowl without disturbing the vegetables too much. Chop some fresh parsley or dill and sprinkle over the top, and serve with lemon wedges on the side for squeezing over.

CAULIFLOWER STEAK

Our friend and fab chef Doug McMaster started the world's first zero-waste restaurant, called Silo, based in Brighton in the UK. When we first visited we were so impressed with Doug and his amazing food that we had to invite him to visit and see what we do. Doug came, and we put on a supper club and a talk in the Happy Pear, which went down really well. This recipe is our take on one of Doug's, and this is what he has to say about it: 'This is a vegan game-changer; its robust meaty quality will convert the most resilient of carnivores. The beauty of the cauliflower "tree of life" presentation makes it the ultimate dinner party showstopper.'

60 MINS

For the mushroom risotto

600g button mushrooms

1½ tablespoons oil

300g short-grain brown rice

2 litres water

a large bunch of fresh thyme

3 tablespoons tamari/soy sauce

2 tablespoons miso paste

For the cauliflower steak

3 medium to large cauliflowers

sea salt

oil

To serve

juice of ½ a lemon

1. The mushroom miso risotto is your first job, as it takes about 30-40 minutes. Roughly slice your mushrooms. Put the oil into a heavy-based pan over a high heat, add the mushrooms and cook for 5 minutes, until they reduce and turn brown. Pour in the rice and the water, and add the leaves from about half your bunch of thyme (pick the leaves off the stalks). Bring to a simmer and leave to boil until the rice is cooked, about 30-40 minutes. It should smell (and taste) very mushroomy.

2. Add the tamari and the miso to make the flavour more intense. The risotto needs to be full of flavour, as the cauliflower has quite neutral flavours.

3. While the rice is cooking, take all the outer leaves off the cauliflowers and reserve for another use. Turn the head of one cauliflower upside down and cut through the centre of the root, directly downwards. Then cut the steak 2½cm from the centre, parallel with your first cut. This will reveal a beautiful 'tree of life' steak. You will get 2 big steaks from one cauliflower. Repeat with the other cauliflowers, reserving all your trims for another use.

continued on next page »

4. Bring a big pan of water to a simmer. Season the water with salt, add the cauliflower steaks and poach until tender. This can be done ahead of time, while your risotto is cooking.

5. Pick the rest of the thyme leaves off their stalks and set aside.

6. When you're nearly ready to serve dinner, take your poached cauliflower steaks, heat a little oil in a pan and fry them on each side on a medium heat until they have picked up a little colour and are heated through.

7. Now it's time to assemble your five-star dinner. It's best to heat up your plates before serving (you might prefer to use shallow bowls). Add a couple of ladles of the risotto and spread it out.

8. Place a cauliflower steak neatly in the centre of each risotto portion and sprinkle the reserved thyme leaves over. Finish by squeezing some lemon juice over each serving.

CHESTNUT & CASHEW WELLINGTON

This was the star of our first full vegan family Christmas, which we had for seventeen members of our family, and it went down a treat. It's a wonderful centrepiece that's delicious and festive when served with our gravy and cranberry sauce. Cooked chestnuts are usually available in vacuum packs around the holiday season.

60 MINS

2 sheets of ready-rolled puff pastry

2 red onions

¼ of a head of a celeriac (approx. 150g)

3 medium carrots (200g)

200g cashew nuts

2 tablespoons sunflower oil, plus extra for brushing the pastry

a small bunch of fresh thyme

a small bunch of fresh sage

100g cooked chestnuts (vacuum-packed)

a pinch of dried cayenne

2 tablespoons tamari/soy sauce

1 teaspoon sea salt

½ teaspoon freshly ground black pepper

150g cooked couscous or quinoa (follow instructions on the pack)

pink peppercorns, to garnish

1. If your pastry is frozen, defrost it – this is best done by removing it from the freezer the night before and putting it into the fridge overnight.

2. Now make the chestnut and cashew filling. Peel and finely slice the onions. Chop any rough gnarly bits off the celeriac and grate it along with the carrots (no need to peel, as a lot of the goodness is in the skin).

3. If your cashew nuts are not roasted, put them into a small pan on a high heat and dry-roast them for about 5-8 minutes, stirring occasionally, till they start to get golden. Set aside to cool down.

4. Put the oil into a large pan or pot on a medium heat. Add the onions and fry for 5 minutes, stirring regularly. Next, add the grated carrots and celeriac, and cook for 5 more minutes, stirring regularly. Remove the pan/pot from the stove.

5. In the meantime, crush two-thirds of your roasted cashew nuts by putting them into a food processor and pulsing until they are finely chopped. If you don't have a food processor, you can wrap them in a tea towel and bash them with a small pan/rolling pin until they are all mashed up and fine.

6. Remove the leaves from the thyme and sage and roughly chop, along with the chestnuts. Add all these to the pot along with the cayenne, tamari, 1 teaspoon of salt and ½ teaspoon of black pepper. Add all the cashew nuts (crushed and uncrushed)

continued on next page »

*1 portion of vegan gravy
(see page 191)*

*1 portion of cranberry sauce
(see page 191)*

and mix well. Taste the filling and season if you think it needs any more salt or pepper.

7. Add the cooked couscous/quinoa to the filling, then put the pot back on the heat and cook for another couple of minutes, stirring well until all is warm and well mixed.

8. Now it's time to assemble your Wellington. Preheat the oven to 180°C/350°F/Gas Mark 4. Line a baking tray with baking parchment. Lay one sheet of puff pastry on the parchment and lightly brush with oil on the top side.

9. Put the cashew and chestnut filling into the centre third of the pastry, leaving a third of the pastry clear on either side and also leaving a little space at each end, so that you can properly seal your Wellington. Form the filling into a smooth mound shape.

10. Place the second sheet of pastry on top, so that it covers the filling completely, and tuck in carefully. Brush the entire outside of the pastry with oil and make score lines with a sharp knife.

11. Bake in the preheated oven for 40 minutes, or until the pastry is golden and puffy and the kitchen smells fab!

12. Before serving, scatter over a few peppercorns if you have them. Serve with cranberry sauce and gravy for a magic meal. Gravy is such a core part of a celebratory dinner that we felt a bit left out as we had none for years, until last year when we came up with the vegan version on page 191. It's quick and easy to make and we reckon it tastes even better than the real thing!

SUNDAY ROAST

Dave was inspired by a vegan Sunday roast he had up in Belfast, so we created this recipe. It really is the full deal – complete with all the trimmings – and is perfect for family gatherings or celebrations. There are a few parts to this dish, so timing is quite important. Start off with roasting the vegetables and prepare your roasted 'meat' in the meantime. The peas will only take a minute to prepare, so leave them until the end, just before serving.

60 MINS

For the roast veg

1kg potatoes

1 teaspoon sea salt

5 tablespoons oil

4 medium carrots

4 medium parsnips

1 tablespoon maple syrup

For the roast 'meat'

150g vital wheat gluten
(see page 116)

4 tablespoons nutritional
yeast

1 teaspoon smoked paprika

1 teaspoon sea salt

½ teaspoon freshly ground
black pepper

1 x 400g tin of cooked lentils

150g oyster mushrooms

100g tomato purée

3 tablespoons tamari/
soy sauce

50ml vegetable stock

1. Preheat the oven to 180°C/350°F/Gas Mark 4.

2. Scrub the potatoes, chop them into halves or quarters and put them into a mixing bowl. Sprinkle over the salt, drizzle over 3 tablespoons of the oil and mix so that all the potatoes are well coated. Spread out on a baking tray, put in the preheated oven and bake for about 45 minutes, or until they are turning golden.

3. While the potatoes are baking, chop the scrubbed carrots and parsnips into batons and pop them into the same mixing bowl you used for the potatoes. Add the remaining 2 tablespoons of oil and the maple syrup, and mix well. Spread out on another baking tray and bake in the oven for 40 minutes, or until they start to char slightly.

4. Now for the main event, the roast! In a clean bowl, mix together the vital wheat gluten, nutritional yeast, smoked paprika, salt and black pepper. Drain and rinse the lentils and leave to dry in a colander. Finely chop the mushrooms, then add them to the bowl along with the lentils and the tomato purée, and mix well. Slowly add the tamari and three-quarters of the stock, and mix well together. You want the mixture to be quite dry.

continued on next page »

*1 portion of vegan gravy
(see page 191)*

1 tablespoon maple syrup

*1 tablespoon tamari/soy
sauce*

2 tablespoons oil

400g frozen peas

5. Add the remaining stock a bit at a time, being careful, as you don't want a wet 'dough'. Knead it with your hands for a couple of minutes, until it comes together into a dough ball.

6. Divide the dough ball into 6-8 pieces. On a board, flatten them out to a rectangle about 3cm thick, making sure they are a suitable size to fit inside your steamer. Set up the steamer over a pot of water and bring the water to the boil. Cut enough pieces of tin foil or parchment paper to wrap fully around each rectangle of dough. Place a piece of foil or parchment on the counter. Wrap your first 'meat' strip, compressing lightly with your hands to give it an even shape, then fold/twist the ends closed so that it is entirely covered. Repeat with the remaining pieces of dough.

7. Place all the wrapped strips in the steamer, cover, and steam for 30 minutes. Remove from the heat and allow to cool slightly before unwrapping. (If you want to pre-make the strips and save time, you can store them in a covered container in the fridge for 3-4 days.)

8. Pour half the vegan gravy into a mixing bowl and add the maple syrup and tamari. Marinate each 'meat' strip in the gravy so that it absorbs as much flavour as possible. Put a flat pan on a high heat and add the oil. Once hot, put in the strips and cook for about 3 minutes on each side, or until each one starts to char and smell amazing! Heat the remainder of the gravy (and any leftover marinade if you like).

9. Now get your peas on. Fill a small saucepan with boiling water and put on a medium heat. Add your peas and boil for 1 minute, then remove and drain in a colander.

10. Serve each plate with a roasted 'meat' slice, a portion of roast potatoes, carrots and parsnips, some peas, and top with hot, steaming gravy!

CRANBERRY SAUCE

This is very easy to make, with the benefit of no refined sugar. Here we use chia seeds to thicken the sauce and give it that cranberry sauce texture. Goes great with the chestnut and cashew Wellington (see page 185).

200g fresh cranberries | *200ml orange juice* | *100ml maple syrup/other liquid sweetener* | *2 tablespoons chia seeds*

1. Put a pan on a high heat and add all the ingredients. Bring to the boil and allow to reduce for a few minutes, stirring occasionally.

2. It's ready when the cranberries have all popped and the sauce is a lovely dark red colour. You can use the back of a wooden spoon to encourage the cranberries to break down.

3. If you want a smooth texture, simply blend with a stick blender or in a food processor/blender.

VEGAN GRAVY

1½ tablespoons oil | *1 onion* | *500ml vegetable stock* | *4 tablespoons nutritional yeast* | *4 tablespoons tamari/soy sauce* | *2 teaspoons garlic powder (or 4 cloves of garlic, super-finely chopped)* | *a pinch of freshly ground black pepper* | *3 tablespoons cornflour* | *4 tablespoons olive oil*

1. Peel and finely chop the onion.

2. Put a small non-stick saucepan on a high heat and add the oil. Once the pan has heated up, add the chopped onion and cook for 2–3 minutes, stirring regularly.

3. Mix the vegetable stock in a large jug with the nutritional yeast, tamari, garlic powder (or finely chopped garlic) and black pepper.

4. Pour the stock mix into the pan and bring to the boil, then reduce the heat down to a gentle simmer. Sift the cornflour into the mix a little at a time, stirring continuously. Then add the olive oil and cook for a further 3–4 minutes.

5. Place a sieve over a 1 litre jug/large bowl and pour through the gravy from the pan. For a thicker consistency and stronger taste, you can leave the mixture to simmer for longer. Enjoy!

HEALTHY EATING ON THE ROAD

When travelling, healthy options can be hard to find and you won't always have time to search for them. However, it's actually pretty easy to keep on track with your healthy eating lifestyle if you just think ahead.

We travel a lot these days, and often the journeys are lengthy, as we're called to London or to the other side of the country for talks, demos and book signings. It's something we enjoy, but it requires a bit of planning as far as us two food monsters are concerned!

When we travel we always bring a food bag. That way we can eat healthily on the move. Generally we pack fresh fruit, wholegrain crackers, hummus, pesto, avocados, dried fruit, nuts and seeds.

We often leave early to catch flights to London, and sometimes joke that people would think we have food hang-ups given the amount of stuff we bring. But by the end of the day generally we wish we had brought more! More is always better when it comes to the amount of provisions you carry – a well-stocked food bag lessens the potential for resorting to the fast food counter or vending machine when the munchies call. It also allows for delays. And being well-fed heads off any travel-induced rage!

Even for family holidays, we always bring basic provisions with us like oats, snacks, spices, and some of the kids' favourites that we might not find en route or at our destination. It's amazing the power that a food bag can have when it comes to ending tantrums and sibling squabbles!

When we make up these bags we are a bit conscious of how neurotic we might look, but it's actually about practicality and convenience. This way we have a no-fuss way of making sure we eat the way we want to eat and don't waste time looking for suitable food when we're on the move.

A FEW MORE TOP TIPS FOR EATING ON THE MOVE:

- **Carry higher-calorie foods!** Calories are another word for energy. Lugging around a bag of low-calorie foods like apples and watermelons, which aren't going to fill you or satisfy your cravings, doesn't make much sense. You need to eat satisfying foods when travelling.

- **Go nuts on nuts!** Nuts are such an easy, nutritious snack. Walnuts and almonds are our favourites. Pair these with dried fruit and you've got yourself a nifty little travel snack that totally trumps chocolate! (Steer clear of roasted salted nuts, as these are more like bar food snacks, akin to crisps, than additions to a healthy lifestyle.)

- **Stop for a picnic if possible!** We'll admit that there's only so much nuts and dried fruit that you can eat before you start to feel like a squirrel! When our tummies start to rumble for something savoury and satisfying, we turn to our quick-fix on-the-go sambo. We make a bit of an occasion of taking a break, chilling and laying out a little picnic with the riches of the food bag - avocados, hummus, pesto and wholegrain crackers.

- **Don't forget utensils!** Plastic knives, forks and spoons will save you from any messy situations.

- **Eat sweet snacks with high nutrition!** Carry energy balls, chocolate salted caramel bites, energy bars and fruit. We might dip any of the above into some nut butter for additional sustenance.

These are just some simple ways that enable us to feel good while on the go, and to continue making healthy eating a priority. If you forget your food bag or it's not convenient to carry one, there's no point in getting stressed out about it. Just do your best to find food that will make you feel good and give you the energy you need while travelling. There are more and more healthier options out there in mainstream outlets.

Also, www.happycow.net is an online directory of vegetarian and vegan restaurants around the world. Star restaurants that you like the sound of in Google Maps on your phone so when you are abroad and get hungry, you will know what is nearby.

Go forth and have happy and healthy travels :)

SUMMER FRUIT BAKEWELL TART ▶ / BLACK FOREST GÂTEAU / DOUBLE-CHOC BROWNIE CAKE / JUMBO

JAFFA CAKE / EASY PUMPKIN PIE ▶ / CHOCOLATEY CHOCOLATE MOUSSE ▶ / CHOCOLATE BISCUIT CAKE /

CRUNCHY CHOC CHIP COOKIES / AMERICAN-STYLE CHOC CHIP COOKIES / FLAPJACKS / CHOCOLATE

CREME COOKIES / HEAVENLY COCONUT BARS / FROZEN CHOC 'N' VANILLA BARS / CHOC JAFFA BALLS /

CHOCOLATE-COATED TRUFFLES / ZESTY HOT CHOCOLATE ▶ / GOLDEN MILK (TURMERIC MILK) ▶

SWEET
TREATS

SUMMER FRUIT BAKEWELL TART

This is a wonderful traditional summer fruit dessert, with shortcrust pastry, a jammy fruit layer and a wonderful delicate almond layer, known as frangipane. For a gluten-free option, just replace the white flour with buckwheat or gluten-free flour.

60 MINS

For the shortcrust pastry

150g white flour/buckwheat flour

75g cold coconut oil

a pinch of sea salt

3-4 tablespoons cold water

For the frangipane

1½ tablespoons ground flax seeds

4 tablespoons water

130g cold coconut oil

155g ground almonds

140ml maple syrup

1¼ teaspoons baking powder

For the jam/fruit layer

250g fresh raspberries/ strawberries

4 tablespoons water

100ml maple syrup

2 tablespoons chia seeds

To decorate

50g flaked almonds

1. Preheat your oven to 180°C/350°F/Gas Mark 4. Line the base of a 23cm springform cake tin with baking parchment.

2. Start by making the pastry. Put the flour into a large mixing bowl. Finely chop the coconut oil and add to the bowl with the salt, then massage with your fingers until the coconut oil has mixed with the flour to form a breadcrumb-like texture with no lumps – about 3 minutes.

3. Add 3 tablespoons of water, and press the mixture together into a firm ball. Add another tablespoon of water if it's not sticking together yet. Wrap the dough in clingfilm and put it into the fridge for 5 minutes to firm up.

4. Lightly coat your hands with flour. Shape the dough into a disc about the size of the springform tin base, and press firmly into the bottom of the tin so that it makes a layer about ½cm thick that evenly covers the whole base, but not the sides.

5. Pop the cake tin into the preheated oven for 10 minutes to blind bake (no need for baking paper and dried beans). Take it out of the oven and place on a rack to cool, leaving the oven turned on.

6. Next, make your frangipane mixture. Put the ground flax seeds and water into a bowl, mix well together and set aside until you have an egg-like consistency. Melt the coconut oil in a small pot over a high heat. Once melted, transfer to a mixing bowl, add the ground almonds, maple syrup, baking powder and the flax egg, and mix until everything is well combined.

7. To make your strawberry or raspberry jam, chop the strawberries finely (no need to chop if using raspberries) and put the fruit into a medium-size pot along with the water. Cook over a medium heat until the fruit starts to break down, which should take a couple of minutes. Add the maple syrup and chia seeds, bring to the boil, then simmer for 6–8 minutes to reduce and thicken. Stir regularly to prevent the jam burning or sticking to the bottom. Remove from the heat, transfer to a bowl and leave to cool and firm up.

8. Cover the cooled base with all the jam. Next, gently spoon the frangipane mixture on top of the jam layer, making sure to cover it all. If any pink or red colour from the fruit comes through the frangipane layer, that's fine – this will make it look more authentic once it's baked. Sprinkle on a layer of flaked almonds.

9. Pop the tart back into the oven and bake for 30 minutes. Once baked, take out and leave to cool for about 15 minutes before slicing and devouring!

BLACK FOREST GÂTEAU

This was always Dave's favourite cake growing up – chocolate sponge with cherry jam, lots of cream, chocolate shavings and cherries on top! This dairy-free version is just as good as his childhood memories. German law dictates that kirsch must be present in a true Black Forest gâteau for it to have that name, so we have included a small amount for authenticity. This is one to make for special occasions.

60 MINS

For the cakes

400g white flour

40g cacao powder

2 teaspoons baking powder

½ teaspoon salt

400ml maple syrup

125ml rice milk/other milk of choice

300ml vegetable oil

1 tablespoon vanilla extract

For the cherry jam/kirsch syrup

1 x 450g tin of black cherries, stoned

2 tablespoons cornflour

4 tablespoons kirsch/cherry brandy/rum (optional)

4 tablespoons maple syrup

For the coconut cream

2 x 400ml tins of full-fat coconut milk

1 tablespoon maple syrup

1 teaspoon vanilla extract

1. Preheat the oven to 180°C/350°F/Gas Mark 4. Line two 23cm springform tins with baking parchment.

2. In a large bowl, sieve the flour, cacao, baking powder and salt to avoid any lumps, and mix. In a separate bowl mix the wet ingredients – the maple syrup, rice milk, vegetable oil and vanilla.

3. Make a well in the centre of the dry ingredients, pour in the wet ingredients and mix well – it should result in a wet brownie batter that is super tasty!

4. Divide the cake batter between the two prepared tins and bake in the preheated oven for 25–30 minutes. Test to see if the cake bases are cooked by inserting a knife or fork into the middle – it should come out clean, but if there is cake batter sticking to it, it needs more time in the oven. Repeat until the knife/fork comes out clean. Remove from the oven and leave to cool completely.

5. While the cakes are in the oven, start the cherry jam and coconut cream.

6. Drain the tinned cherries, ensuring you keep all the syrup. In a blender, blend half the drained cherries from the can with 120ml of the cherry syrup from the tin, 2 tablespoons of cornflour, 2 tablespoons of kirsch/cherry brandy/rum and 4 tablespoons of maple syrup to make a cherry jam. Blend till smooth, then pour into a saucepan, bring to the boil and let it reduce for 10 minutes, until it becomes jam like. Pour into a bowl and leave to cool and thicken.

For the topping

50g dark chocolate

100g fresh cherries (if none available, use another tin of black cherries for garnish)

7. Now make the cream. Open both tins of coconut milk and scoop off the coconut cream from the top, leaving the water behind. Put the cream into a mixing bowl and whisk together with the maple syrup and vanilla extract. Set aside until you are ready to assemble your gâteau.

8. Mix 4 tablespoons of the cherry syrup from the tin with the remaining 2 tablespoons of kirsch in a jug. Lightly pierce the two cake bases with a skewer, then pour the cherry/kirsch liquid evenly over the top of both cakes. Leave them to cool fully.

9. Once fully cooled, spread the cherry jam on top of one of the cakes. Next, layer on the rest of the tinned cherries and lastly spread over half the coconut cream.

10. Carefully place the second cake on top and cover with the remaining coconut cream. With a microplane grater or fine grater, grate some chocolate on top. Decorate with cherries and enjoy this wonderful cake!

DOUBLE-CHOC BROWNIE CAKE

This started out as a quick indulgent dessert for Steve's son Theo's birthday, and it went down so well that we decided to experiment with it. Chocolate mousse in the middle and on top makes it even more of a party cake!

45 MINS

For the cake

100g ground almonds

150g white flour

2 teaspoons baking powder

25g cacao powder

1 teaspoon sea salt

150g coconut oil

250ml maple syrup

50ml rice milk

1 tablespoon vanilla extract

For the chocolate mousse icing

cold water

a handful of ice

200g dark chocolate

150ml boiling water

For the filling

100g yoghurt of choice (we like coconut)

125g fresh raspberries

1. Preheat the oven to 160°C/325°F/Gas Mark 3. Line a brownie tray/high-sided baking tray with baking parchment.

2. Sift the ground almonds, flour, baking powder, cacao powder and salt into a large mixing bowl, and stir everything together.

3. Melt the coconut oil in a small saucepan over a high heat. Remove from the heat and add the maple syrup, rice milk and vanilla extract. Mix well, then make a well in the centre of the dry ingredients and pour in the wet ingredients from the saucepan. Mix well – it should result in a very wet brownie batter.

4. Pour the brownie batter into your prepared tin so that it is about 3cm deep, and bake in the preheated oven for 25 minutes. Remove and leave to cool.

5. Now make the chocolate mousse. Get two metal or plastic bowls, one a bit smaller than the other one. Into the larger one, put the handful of ice and about the same volume of cold water.

6. Chop the dark chocolate into small pieces, put into the second bowl and pour the boiling water over. Using a whisk, stir continuously until the chocolate has all melted and it's like a hot chocolate.

7. Take the bowl of melted chocolate and place this bowl inside the bowl of ice and water. Stir continuously for 3–5 minutes. The ice bath lowers the temperature of the chocolate, allowing the cacao butter to harden and emulsify with the water, resulting in an amazing moussey texture! Stir until the chocolate sticks to the whisk without falling when you hold it above the bowl.

8. Next, take the cooled cake and cut into 8 similar-size brownies. Place 4 brownies on a plate to make the base of the cake, ensuring they are all touching in the middle. Spread half the chocolate mousse on top of these. If the mousse is too thick, add a little more boiling water to give it more of a buttery texture.

9. Next, spread the yoghurt on top of the chocolate mousse and evenly distribute half the raspberries on top. Place the remaining 4 brownies on top of that, again ensuring they are all touching in the middle. Cover with the remaining chocolate mousse and top with the rest of the raspberries. Cut into smaller brownie cake bites, or leave as large brownie cake portions.

JUMBO JAFFA CAKE

Growing up we loved eating Jaffa Cakes as treats. Here is our whole-food based alternative – and while we were at it we super-sized it and turned it into a cake!

60 MINS

For the base

250g coconut oil

200g ground almonds

200g white spelt flour/white flour

350ml maple syrup/agave syrup

3 teaspoons baking powder

1 teaspoon sea salt

50ml milk of choice

1½ tablespoons vanilla extract

For the orange jelly

3 organic oranges

250ml maple syrup

3½ teaspoons agar agar flakes

For the topping

200g dark chocolate

50g coconut oil (to soften the chocolate for ease of cutting)

1. Preheat your oven to 160°C/325°F/Gas Mark 3. Line the base of a 23cm springform cake tin with baking parchment.

2. To make the base, melt the oil in a medium pot over a high heat, then pour into a large bowl.

3. Add all the other base ingredients to the bowl and mix or whisk until the batter is evenly mixed. Pour into the prepared springform tin and bake in the preheated oven for 40 minutes.

4. Test that it is properly done by sticking in a skewer – it should come out dry. When the cake is ready, run a knife around the edge of the tin, remove the cake and place on a rack to cool completely.

5. Now make the orange jelly. Peel and roughly chop the oranges and put them into a medium-size pan over a medium heat with the maple syrup and agar agar flakes. Bring to the boil, then reduce the heat and simmer for 10 minutes, until the oranges are soft, mashing the mixture occasionally with a spoon.

6. Sieve the orangey mixture into a bowl and leave to cool for 10-15 minutes. Once it has set into a jelly, spoon it on top of the base.

7. Make the topping by melting the chocolate and coconut oil in a heatproof bowl set over a pan of gently simmering water. Pour this over your orange jelly layer and leave to cool. Before slicing this cake, it's best to heat your knife by running it under the hot tap and wiping dry. When the blade is hot, the chocolate will not crack and you'll get lovely smooth edges to your slices.

EASY PUMPKIN PIE

This is a quick and easy favourite of ours, and it has the most gorgeous orange colour. To roast a pumpkin, simply chop it up, put it on a baking tray, and bake in a preheated 180°C/350°F/Gas Mark 4 oven for 30 minutes.

70 MINS

For the base

300g nuts (almonds/ walnuts/cashews)

100g pitted dates

2 tablespoons coconut oil

1 teaspoon vanilla extract

For the pumpkin filling

150g cashew nuts

175g roasted pumpkin or pumpkin purée (from a tin)

150g coconut oil

80ml maple syrup

50g chopped pitted dates

½ teaspoon ground cinnamon

1 teaspoon ground ginger

For the topping

a handful of pecan nuts, chopped

2 tablespoons maple syrup

1. Line a 23cm springform cake tin with baking parchment. Soak the cashew nuts for the filling in a bowl of warm water.

2. Blitz the nuts for the base in a food processor until they resemble breadcrumbs. Add the rest of the base ingredients and blend until they start to come together (2–3 minutes). Spread this over the base of your springform tin and compact it down with the back of a spoon so that it really stays together. Pop this into the fridge while you make your pumpkin filling.

3. Drain and rinse the cashew nuts, then transfer to a food processor. Add the rest of the pumpkin filling ingredients and blend until the mixture is smooth. This should take about 5 minutes. When it is ready, spread this mixture evenly on top of your nutty base layer. Put back in the fridge for about an hour to set.

4. Meanwhile, make your topping by toasting the pecans in a dry pan on a medium heat with the maple syrup, to caramelize them. This should take about 5–8 minutes – make sure you stir them regularly to avoid them burning. Sprinkle them on top of your pie when it comes out of the fridge – it will really take it to the next level! Cut around the edges of the tin with a sharp knife to ensure the pie doesn't stick to the sides. Carefully remove from the tin, slice and enjoy!

CHOCOLATEY CHOCOLATE MOUSSE

We first came across this most chocolatey chocolate mousse ever in our friend Doug McMaster's restaurant, Silo, in Brighton. We asked what was in it, expecting to hear cream, but to our surprise it contained only chocolate and water.

5–10 MINS

cold water

a handful of ice

150ml boiling water

200g dark chocolate

1. Put equal parts of cold water and ice into a medium metal or plastic bowl to create an ice bath.

2. Boil the kettle and pour 150ml of boiling water into a second medium (ideally metal) bowl. This bowl needs to fit inside the bowl with the ice bath.

3. Chop the chocolate into small pieces and add to the bowl of boiling water. Stir with a spatula or whisk until all the pieces are melted and it has the texture and smoothness of a hot chocolate.

4. Place the bowl of chocolate over the ice bath, with the bottom of the bowl touching the ice-cold water, and whisk vigorously. Continue to whisk until the mixture has the consistency of stiff whipped cream, about 3–5 minutes.

5. If it gets too thick, don't worry, just add a little more boiling water and mix it in. Best kept in the fridge. Enjoy on its own, dip fruit in it or use it as icing on a cake.

CHOCOLATE BISCUIT CAKE

One of our childhood favourites, this is a wonderfully indulgent cake that always satisfies the most chocolatey of itches! This is a simple recipe and a total crowd-pleaser. If you don't have time to bake your own cookies, simply use your favourite store-bought chocolate chip cookies.

200g chocolate chip cookies (use the healthier choc chip cookie recipe on page 214)

200g dark chocolate

100g coconut oil

100ml maple syrup

50g walnuts

20–30 MINS

1. Preheat the oven to 120°C/250°F/Gas Mark ½ and line a 900g loaf tin with baking parchment.

2. To get the crunchiest biscuit bite in this cake, you need to double-bake your cookies. Break them into small chunks, place on a baking tray and bake in the preheated oven for 20 minutes.

3. While they are in the oven, put the dark chocolate and coconut oil into a bowl over a pan of simmering water and let them melt. Once melted, remove from the heat and stir in the maple syrup. Leave the bowl over the pan of hot water to keep it liquid.

4. Once the cookies are double-baked, remove from the oven and leave them to cool fully. Transfer the cooled cookie pieces to your prepared loaf tin.

5. Roughly chop the walnuts into small bite-size pieces and add to the cookie pieces in the tin. Pour the chocolate over them and spread so that all the cookies are covered.

6. Leave to cool, then put into the fridge to harden. Remove from the fridge a few minutes before you want to slice it.

CRUNCHY CHOC CHIP COOKIES

These are crumbly, chewy, super-satisfying, quick and reasonably easy to make, a blend between a cookie and a flapjack, and well worth the effort! The oat flour and ground almonds give the cookies more of a crunchy bite, as well as more fibre!

30 MINS

70g rolled oats

1 tablespoon ground flax seeds

3 tablespoons water

100g coconut oil

100g coconut sugar/caster sugar/brown sugar

70g white flour

60g ground almonds

1 teaspoon baking powder

70g good-quality dark or milk chocolate chips

1. Preheat the oven to 160°C/325°F/Gas Mark 3 and line two baking trays with baking parchment.

2. Put the oats into a blender and whiz until they reach a flour-like texture. Make a flax egg by mixing the flax seeds and water in a small bowl and leaving to soak for 3–4 minutes.

3. In another (medium-size) bowl, beat together the coconut oil and sugar using a fork until it becomes smooth and almost creamy (1–2 minutes). Add the flax egg to this mixture and beat everything together.

4. Now add the oat flour from the blender, the white flour, ground almonds and baking powder, mixing well until there are no lumps. Lastly, stir in three-quarters of the chocolate chips.

5. Form the dough into a ball, and, if you have time, wrap it in clingfilm and refrigerate for 10–20 minutes – this will make it easier to shape into cookies.

6. Divide the dough into 12 golfball-size balls. Flatten each one by pressing down with the back of a spoon, and push the remaining chocolate chips into the top surface of each one. Place on the prepared baking trays.

7. Bake in the preheated oven for 18 minutes, until they start to turn lightly golden. Remove from the oven and leave to cool until they are cool enough to touch = eat. They will keep in an airtight container for up to 2 weeks.

AMERICAN-STYLE CHOC CHIP COOKIES

These are based on a more traditional American-style choc chip cookie. If you want to make them healthier, substitute wholemeal flour for the white flour.

25 MINS

½ tablespoon ground flax seeds

1½ tablespoons water

85g coconut oil

110g coconut sugar/ brown sugar

1 teaspoon vanilla extract

125g white flour/wholemeal flour

a pinch of sea salt

⅓ teaspoon bicarbonate of soda

70g good-quality chocolate chips

1. Preheat the oven to 160°C/325°F/Gas Mark 3 and line two baking trays with baking parchment.

2. First make a flax egg by mixing the ground flax seeds and water together and leaving to soak for 3-4 minutes.

3. In a large bowl, beat the coconut oil and sugar together using a fork and wooden spoon until well combined. Add the vanilla extract, followed by the flax egg, and beat in well.

4. Sift in the flour, salt and bicarbonate of soda and mix until everything comes together into a dough. Take care not to overwork the dough, as this can develop gluten.

5. Fold in three-quarters of the chocolate chips, and ideally wrap the dough in clingfilm and refrigerate for 10–20 minutes – this will make your cookies easier to shape.

6. Divide the mixture into 12 golfball-size balls, spacing them well apart. Flatten each one by pressing down with the back of a spoon, then push the remaining chocolate chips into the top surface of each one. Divide between the prepared baking trays.

7. Bake in the preheated oven for 12–15 minutes, until golden. Cool on the trays, then store in an airtight container for up to 2 weeks.

FLAPJACKS

These crunchy, chewy, superfood-packed, colourful flapjacks are a real indulgence. We first created them with our friend Simon in London, and they quickly became a treat in Steve's house with the little pears! It is worth getting cocoa butter, as it will result in a firmer flapjack, but if not, coconut oil will work fine.

25 MINS

50g dried apricots

50g dried mango

100g pumpkin seeds

50g desiccated coconut

70g chia seeds

100g walnuts

100g pitted dates

50g goji berries

1 teaspoon vanilla extract

70g cocoa butter/coconut oil

200g dark chocolate

1. Finely chop the dried apricots and mango into small pieces to make it easier on your food processor. Put them into the processor with the pumpkin seeds, coconut, chia seeds, walnuts, dates, goji berries and vanilla extract, and pulse until the nuts and seeds are well chopped and broken up but there is still some texture to them. Pour the blended mixture into a large bowl.

2. Melt the cocoa butter in a bowl over simmering water, the same as you would melt chocolate. Once melted, pour it over the nut and seed mixture and mix well.

3. Line a flapjack tray with baking parchment and spread the mixture evenly so that it is about 3cm thick. Using the back of a spoon, smooth the top level.

4. Now melt the chocolate in the bowl over simmering water and spread over the nut and seed mixture.

5. Put into the fridge and leave for 20 minutes to set. Once cooled, chop into 4 x 4 pieces, to make 16 flapjack bars. Store in an airtight tin for up to a week.

CHOCOLATE CREME COOKIES

Here is a simple, delicious and healthy take on the popular Oreo™ cookie. These take about 10 minutes to make and are dairy and gluten free.

20 MINS

For the cookies

100g almonds

100g cashew nuts

125g pitted dates

1 teaspoon vanilla extract

a pinch of sea salt

3 tablespoons raw cacao powder

1 tablespoon maple syrup

For the creamy filling

100g raw cashew nuts/ cashew nut butter

2 tablespoons coconut oil

3 tablespoons agave syrup/ liquid sweetener of choice (ideally a clear liquid, as we want the filling to be white)

1 teaspoon vanilla extract

1. If you are using cashew nuts for the filling, ideally soak them overnight. If you don't have time, simply soak them for 5 minutes in boiling water. Alternatively, you can use cashew nut butter, which will also result in a creamy texture.

2. In a food processor, blend the almonds and cashew nuts for 3 minutes, until they become smooth and breadcrumb-like. Add the dates, vanilla extract, salt, cacao powder and maple syrup, and blend until everything is well mixed.

3. Spread a large piece of baking parchment on the counter and pour the mixture on to it. Using a rolling pin or clean jar, roll out the mixture so that it is ½–1cm thick. A top tip to make it easier to roll is to fold half of the baking parchment over the top of the cookie mixture and roll over it to prevent sticking.

4. Get a smooth-rimmed cookie cutter about 5cm in diameter. Cut out 20–28 cookies, using all the mixture, which will work out at 10–14 finished cookie sandwiches – you need an even number! Leave aside while you make the filling.

5. Put the soaked (and drained) cashew nuts or the cashew nut butter into a blender with the coconut oil, agave syrup and vanilla extract, and blend for 3–5 minutes, until you get a super-smooth, creamy texture.

6. To finish your cookies, simply put a generous teaspoon of the filling on top of one of the cookie bases and top with another cookie. Repeat with the rest of the cookies. These will keep in an airtight container for up to 2 weeks.

HEAVENLY COCONUT BARS

Growing up, Bounty Bars™ were always Dave's favourite chocolate bars, so it was important that we created something equally delicious! These are really easy to make, and as they are dairy and gluten free they're perfect for everyone. This recipe makes about 18 small bars, which might seem like a lot, but you'll be surprised how quickly they disappear!

45 MINS

3 tablespoons coconut oil

4 tablespoons maple syrup

1 teaspoon vanilla extract

200g desiccated coconut

75g ground almonds

a small pinch of sea salt

250–300g dark chocolate

1. Put a medium-size pot on a medium heat and add the coconut oil, maple syrup and vanilla extract. Heat until the coconut oil has melted, ensuring the liquid does not boil.

2. Put the desiccated coconut, ground almonds and salt into a mixing bowl and mix well. Once the coconut oil has melted, add the heated liquid to the bowl and mix thoroughly.

3. Place some baking parchment on a baking tray and spread the coconut mixture over it. Shape the mixture into a square shape roughly 20cm x 20cm and 2½cm thick.

4. Place the baking tray in the freezer for 20 minutes, for the mixture to harden. After 20 minutes, the coconut bars should be firm enough to cut into solid bar shapes. You should get about 18 small bars.

5. Next up . . . chocolate time! Place your dark chocolate in a glass or metal bowl and melt it over a pot of gently simmering water, stirring occasionally until it fully melts. Remove from the heat.

6. Time to give the coconut bars a chocolate bath! We have found the best way to cover them in chocolate is to place a bar on a palette knife or large knife and pour the chocolate over the bar with a spoon or ladle until fully coated. Try to avoid dropping the coconut bars into the

chocolate, as they will melt and make your chocolate lumpy with coconut. Put a little chocolate on the bottom, repeat and leave to harden. If you want ridged lines on the top of the bars, use a fork while the chocolate is still soft. It will most likely take a few goes to get this right, but it is fun to practise!

7. Place the now coated bars on fresh parchment paper on a baking tray and pop them into the fridge for 10-15 minutes, to allow the chocolate to cool and harden.

FROZEN CHOC 'N' VANILLA BARS

We have a strong emotional connection to Milky Ways™ as they were a favourite Friday night treat our Dad gave us when we were kids! This tribute to our childhood favourite is really fun, easy to make and oh so tasty. These are fantastic served straight from the freezer, almost like a chocolate-coated ice cream bar – the shell is cold and crisp and the inside is gooey with a fab vanilla flavour.

250ml soya milk

1 teaspoon vanilla extract

100ml maple syrup

350ml sunflower oil

4 teaspoons tapioca flour/
   rice flour/cornflour

200g dark chocolate

30 MINS PREP

1. Put the soya milk into a blender (don't substitute any other milk, as it won't work to emulsify the liquids). Add the vanilla extract and maple syrup, and blend until well combined.

2. With the blender running at a slow speed, slowly add the sunflower oil through the hole in the lid. Continue to blend on a low speed until it emulsifies and has the consistency of a thick custard or mayonnaise.

3. Pour the mixture into a small saucepan on a low heat. Sift in the tapioca, stirring continuously. Heat to a gentle simmer, then turn off the heat – you don't want it to boil. As it cools down, it will bind together more.

4. Spread the mixture in a parchment-lined flapjack tray, making an even layer about 2cm thick. Cover the tray with clingfilm and put into the freezer overnight.

5. Remove from the freezer and cut into even-size bars about 8–10cm x 3–4cm. Melt the chocolate in a heatproof bowl over a pan of gently simmering water. To coat the bars in the melted chocolate, put each one on a palette knife or large knife and pour the melted chocolate over with a spoon or ladle until it properly coats each side of the bar.

6. Leave to set in the freezer – these work best served straight from the freezer, as the chocolate will have a great bite and the inside will be lovely and gooey.

CHOC JAFFA BALLS

Light and chocolatey, these make a great treat and are perfect for kids' lunchboxes or for that mid-afternoon slump when you are looking for something sweet. Lovely on their own, or even spread on toast!

20 MINS

200g pitted dates

75ml orange juice

80g oats

120g cashew nuts

2 tablespoons cacao powder

zest of ½ an orange

For the coating (choose your favourite!)

50g desiccated coconut

100g dark chocolate, melted

25g desiccated coconut +
  zest of ½ an orange +
  1 tablespoon freeze-dried
  raspberry powder

1. Chop the dates into small pieces and soak them in the orange juice for a few minutes, turning them around so that they are all submerged in the juice.

2. Pulse the oats and cashew nuts in a food processor for 30 seconds. Add the soaked dates with the orange juice, then add the cacao powder and the orange zest. Blend all the ingredients until the mix has a smooth texture – about 2 minutes.

3. Roll the mixture into small balls about the size of a small Brussels sprout, and coat each one in your favourite coating. Roll the balls in the coconut for the first option and dip them in melted chocolate for the second (leaving them to harden). For the third option, mix all the ingredients in a bowl and cover each ball for a fab hot pink colour!

4. Store in the fridge for up to a month.

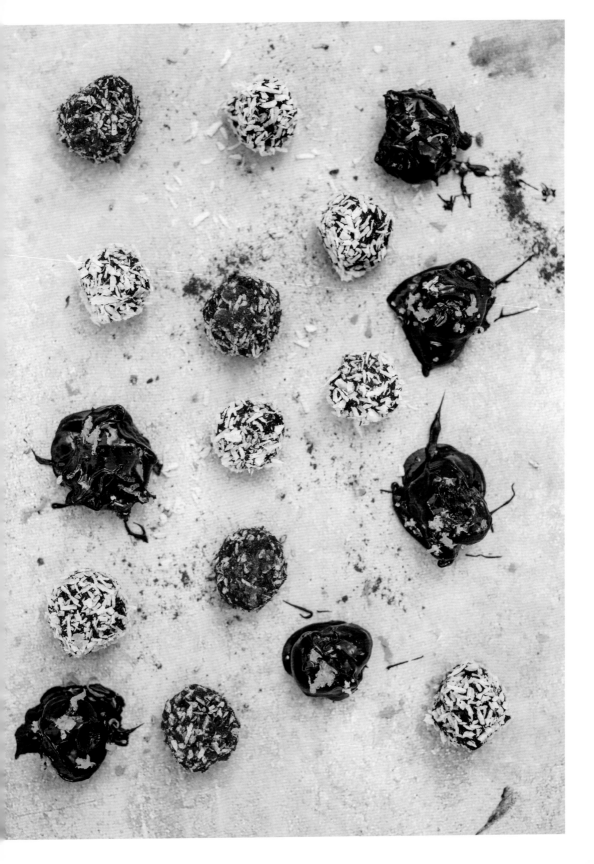

CHOCOLATE-COATED TRUFFLES

These were inspired by Rolos™ and we think they taste as good as the real thing! They're lower in fat, higher in fibre, super-tasty and really easy to make. Make a batch of them as a homemade present.

20 MINS

For the filling

200g Medjool dates

100g walnuts

100g cashew nuts

1 tablespoon coconut oil

1 teaspoon vanilla extract

1 tablespoon cacao powder

For the chocolate coating

250g dark chocolate

dried rose petals/freeze-dried raspberries (optional, for decoration)

1. Stone the dates and put them into a food processor along with the rest of the filling ingredients. Whiz for a few minutes, until super-smooth, like toffee.

2. Remove the filling from the food processor and roll into around 25 balls. Alternatively, flatten out the filling so that it is 1cm thick and use a knife or cutter/mould to cut out 15 heart shapes. Leave to cool.

3. Melt your chocolate in a heatproof bowl set over a pan of barely simmering water. With the help of two spoons, dunk your truffles in the chocolate to fully coat them. Set aside on a sheet of baking parchment until the chocolate hardens.

4. Decorate with dried rose petals or freeze-dried raspberries for a colourful presentation.

ZESTY HOT CHOCOLATE

This drink is like a warm belly hug on a cold evening. The orange zest makes it really special. If you're a mint lover, though, it's worth seeking out some mint oil.

5 MINS

300ml rice milk/other milk of choice

2 tablespoons cacao powder

1 teaspoon vanilla extract

2 tablespoons maple syrup/ other liquid sweetener

2 tablespoons smooth almond butter (use chunky if you prefer chunks!)

zest of ½ an orange, or ½ teaspoon mint oil (optional)

1. Place a saucepan on a medium heat and pour in the milk. Slowly add the rest of the ingredients, along with a tiny pinch of sea salt.

2. Heat the liquid, whisking continuously until the mixture is smooth, creamy and to the temperature you would like. Sip and feel warm right down to your toes.

GOLDEN MILK (TURMERIC MILK)

This sweet, aromatic 'golden milk' is an anti-inflammatory juice, harnessing the health properties of the mighty turmeric, renowned for being antioxidant and arthritis-busting.

5 MINS

500ml rice milk

½ tablespoon maple syrup

1 teaspoon coconut oil

1 teaspoon ground turmeric (or fresh turmeric, finely grated)

2 cinnamon sticks

½ teaspoon ground ginger

4 cardamom pods

2 star anise

a small pinch of black pepper

1. Simply put all the ingredients into a small saucepan on a low to medium heat and bring to a gentle boil, whisking to combine. Once boiled, your milk is ready to go.

2. Serve with a sprinkle of cacao powder or ground cinnamon, or with a star anise on top.

PART II
LIVING HAPPY

We have designed our two-week health reboot so you can dip your toe into the world of healthier eating. Think of it as an experiment – a culinary adventure with really exciting and positive side-effects. Once you try this challenge and experience how easy it is to gain control over your health, weight and energy, we believe you won't want to return to your former habits. Why? Because you'll be eating delicious food, you won't be hungry and you will look and feel SO GOOD!

From our years running the Happy Heart health and wellness courses, in classrooms and online, we've realized that the key to making changes is to provide an easy-to-follow, delicious, food-led programme that isn't time-consuming or expensive. So we've made this as easy as possible – with guidelines, plans and a budget-friendly shopping list that will keep you on the straight and narrow for the next two weeks.

YOUR TWO-WEEK HEALTH REBOOT!

THE TEN GOLDEN RULES

As with every challenge, there are rules to be followed in order to get the results you want. Do your best with our ten golden rules below, but if you slip up, just start over with even stronger resolve.

1. Eat only whole plant foods – fruit, veg, beans, whole grains, nuts and seeds.

2. Don't eat processed foods (refined foods, e.g croissants, cornflakes, etc.).

3. Avoid all meat and dairy products (yes, including eggs!).

4. Don't over-indulge in nuts and avocados (they are healthy, but high in fat, something to be aware of if you're trying to lose weight).

5. Limit the use of oils (see point 4 – oil = fat!).

6. Limit or eliminate alcohol. However, it's not a deal-breaker – if a glass of wine will help you to eat a healthy dinner, then have it!

7. Limit your caffeine intake to either 1–2 cups of coffee per day or 2–3 cups of breakfast/green tea per day. Change all other teas to herbal tea or warm water.

8. Use only dairy-free milk, such as almond, rice, oat, etc.

9. Eat as much as you want, provided the food fits into the food rules. There are no excuses for feeling hungry, just eat more!

10. Don't count calories!

And before you begin . . .

Do a big clear-out! Before you start, clear out your cupboards. Let's face it, when you're feeling tired or down, chocolate and crisps are tempting, so best to either bin them or give them to someone else. Instead, fill your cupboards with healthy options.

Rope in a friend! It can make it easier if you can get someone to do this with you, to motivate each other, and share the ups and downs (and even some of the cooking if they're nearby). It could even be a friend living in a different country.

Plan to log what you eat! From years doing our Happy Heart course, we've found that food journals help people to hold themselves accountable. It's a daily record, for your eyes only, of what you eat and when. There's something about writing things down that stops you in your tracks – after all, you can't very well write down 'one biscuit' if you've eaten half a pack! You know you're cheating and you know that the only one you're cheating is yourself. So keep a journal, either in a notebook, or as a note on your phone.

WEEKLY MEAL PREP

So here it is – the crux of this two-week reboot! We've saved you loads of time and work in figuring out what to buy and cook. In the next few pages there are shopping lists for three different weekly meal plans: one for each of the next two weeks and a third as a bonus. Simply take a photo of the shopping lists on your phone, stock up, then follow the recipes, which are all in this book.

It should take you just an hour to prep your food for the full week. The info is designed for one person and the budget (excluding condiments and store-cupboard basics like salt, spices, tamari, etc.) is under €25/£22 for the week – yes, you can eat a week's worth of delicious, healthy meals for about €3.50/£3 per day! If you don't have some of the store-cupboard basics we mention, that will increase the cost of stocking up at the outset, but most of these will last for weeks or even months.

- The plans cover one person for a full week – breakfast, lunch and dinner. Snacks have not been factored in, but you can look on page 242 for snack ideas. If you're a big eater you will need to stock up on snacks.

- You will need to freeze some dishes, so make room in the freezer!

- Be sure to have enough containers for each meal during the week (you will need about 14).

- To save time when doing the prep, have a few pots on the go at the same time.

- Keeping it simple is at the heart of the reboot, so we don't suggest different meals for every lunch and dinner. There is one breakfast option (see next point!) and two lunch and two dinner options each week. It's up to you if you want to alternate lunches and dinners or have the same thing every day. Either way, they're delicious, and over such a short period of time you won't get bored. Dinner recipes will make eight portions in total, so you always have one left over for another week!

- It's our favourite – porridge – for breakfast in all three plans. Pimp it up with other bits from your cupboard, e.g. fresh fruit, nuts, raisins, a drizzle of maple syrup, toasted seeds (toppings are not in the budget/shopping list – just make sure your toppings follow the rules).

MEAL PREP 1

LUNCH

Leek and potato soup - 4 portions
(page 46)

Or

Toasted wholemeal pitta breads
with hummus

DINNER:

Go-to dahl - 4 portions (page 74)

Three-bean chilli - 4 portions (page 90)

Shopping list:

Fruit and veg

- 1 lemon
- 2 limes
- 1½ bunches of scallions
- 10-15 cherry tomatoes
- a handful of baby spinach
- 1 red chilli
- 1 yellow pepper
- 1 medium onion
- 1 head of garlic
- 600g potatoes
- 600g leeks
- a thumb-size piece of fresh ginger

Other ingredients

- 2 x 400g tins of chickpeas
- 1 x 400g tin of cooked lentils
  (we usually use green ones)
- 1 x 400g tin of kidney beans
- 1 x 400g tin of butter beans
- 1 x 400ml tin of coconut milk
- wholemeal pitta breads
- 2 x 400g tins of chopped tomatoes
- 6 tablespoons tomato purée (100g)
- 200g tub of hummus (x 2 if you plan to
  have hummus for lunch every day)

Spices & condiments (outside budget)

- 5 tablespoons oil
- 4 teaspoons sea salt
- 1 bay leaf
- 2 litres vegetable stock
- 1½ teaspoons black pepper
- 2 tablespoons curry powder
- 4 teaspoons ground cumin
- 3 tablespoons tamari/soy sauce
- 1 tablespoon maple syrup
- 2 teaspoons ground coriander
- ½ teaspoon smoked paprika
- chilli flakes

Extras that go well (outside budget)

- fresh coriander
- plain soya yoghurt (for chilli)
- 100% wholemeal bread (for soup)

Check out our YouTube channel, 'Meal
prep 7 days for €25 under an hour'.

MEAL PREP 2

Simple tomato soup – 4 portions
(page 49)

Toasted wholemeal pitta breads with
hummus

DINNER

Chickpea & aubergine curry – 4
portions (page 65)

One-pot creamy mushroom pasta – 4
portions (page 85)

Shopping list:

Fruit and veg

- 4 onions (1 red)
- 1 head of garlic
- a thumb-size piece of fresh ginger
- 1 fresh red chilli
- 400g mushrooms
- 2 carrots
- 2 medium potatoes
- 1 aubergine
- a decent bunch of fresh basil
  (for both pasta and curry)
- a few sprigs of fresh thyme
- 1 lemon

Other ingredients

- 200ml white wine
- 1 x 400g tin of chickpeas

- 1 x 400ml tin of coconut milk
- 3 x 400g tins of chopped tomatoes
- 500g wholemeal/spelt spaghetti
- 800ml oat milk (or other non-dairy
  milk)
- 200g tub of hummus (x 2 if you plan
  to have hummus for lunch every day)
- wholemeal pitta breads
- small bunch of fresh coriander

Spices and condiments (outside budget)

- 4 teaspoons sea salt
- 1½ teaspoons ground black pepper
- 1.5 litres vegetable stock
- 1 tablespoon maple syrup
- 3 tablespoons tamari/soy sauce
- 2 tablespoons curry powder
- 5 tablespoons oil
- 2 tablespoons nutritional yeast

MEAL PREP 3

Sweet potato coconut chilli
soup - 4 portions (page 50)

Toasted wholemeal pitta breads
with hummus

Easy three-bean sweet potato &
coconut curry - 4 portions (page 70)

One pot spag bol - 4 portions (page 78)

Shopping list:

Fruit and veg

- ⊘ 4 onions (2 red)
- ⊘ 1 head of garlic
- ⊘ 1 red chilli
- ⊘ 1 green chilli
- ⊘ 2 carrots
- ⊘ 1 stick of celery
- ⊘ 1 courgette
- ⊘ 1 lemon
- ⊘ a bunch of fresh basil
- ⊘ 3 sweet potatoes
- ⊘ 1 pack of baby spinach
- ⊘ handful of cherry tomatoes

Other ingredients

- ⊘ 1 x 400g tin of chopped tomatoes
- ⊘ 1 x 400g tin of cooked lentils

- ⊘ 400g wholemeal spaghetti
- ⊘ 1 x 400g tin of butter beans
- ⊘ 1 x 400g tin of black beans
- ⊘ 1 x 400g tin of chickpeas
- ⊘ 2 x 400ml tins of coconut milk
- ⊘ 200g tub of hummus (x 2 if you plan to have hummus for lunch every day)
- ⊘ wholemeal pitta breads

**Spices and condiments
(outside budget)**

- ⊘ 2.6 litres vegetable stock
- ⊘ 3 tablespoons tamari/soy sauce
- ⊘ 4½ tablespoons olive oil
- ⊘ nutritional yeast
- ⊘ 2 tablespoons curry powder
- ⊘ salt and ground black pepper

SNACKING

We love snacking, and have become experts at keeping 'h'anger' at bay (h'anger = being angry and irritable because you're hungry!). When it comes to snacking, we're all about quick and easy foods that satisfy our cravings. Come mid-afternoon, we'd rarely go for anything that requires a recipe because, like most people, we don't have time to start cooking. So here are some super-simple snack ideas:

- Hummus, cucumber, tomato on toasted pittas or wholegrain crackers (Ryvita is one of our favourites and is cheap and widely available).

- Spread hummus on a cracker/rice cake. Top with chopped avocado, a drizzle of lime juice, a pinch of sea salt and black pepper, some chilli flakes and away you go!

- Make a simple trail mix, basing it around seeds, dried fruit, nuts and even some cacao nibs. Keep in a Tupperware container and decant into a small bag to take with you when you're out and about.

- Hummus and carrot or celery sticks.

Of course, sometimes you have a craving for something sweet! Here are some of our favourite go-to snacks when we want a hit of sweetness. Basing these around whole foods means we get plenty of fibre to slow down the release of sugar, while still satisfying our desire for sweet.

- Fresh fruit. Fruit is the perfect fast food, as it's low in calories yet high in fibre and nutrition and needs no prep.

- Rice cakes with hummus/sugar-free jam/banana.

- Dates, pitted (we love Medjool dates) and stuffed with nut butter or a couple of almonds.

- Dried fruit with pumpkin/sunflower seeds. There is more dried fruit out there than raisins! Try some of these: dates and prunes, dried mango, figs, papaya, banana, pineapple or apricots (unsulphured if you can get them). Dried fruit gets a bad rap because it's high in sugar, but it's also high in fibre, so the release of these sugars is much slower than the vast majority of snack bars, which is better for you.

- Choc Jaffa balls (page 224) – make a batch of these and they'll last at least a week.

- Spread rice cakes with tahini and drizzle with a little liquid sweetener such as maple syrup.

- Pre-make our healthy pancake batter (page 21) and keep it covered in a Tupperware container in the fridge, to cook up a batch whenever you feel like it. Serve with banana/mango/a drizzle of maple syrup/soya yoghurt and some cocoa nibs.

- Dunk fruit – such as chunks of banana or apple slices – into tahini or almond butter (eat the almond butter/tahini sparingly, as it is higher in calories and very easy to eat!).

- Chop an apple, top with nut butter and a dollop of coconut yoghurt (or any non-dairy yoghurt of choice) – and once again try to be sparing with the nut butter and coconut yoghurt, as both are higher in fat.

- Nuts and dried fruit go great together. A fave of Steve's is to make a 'fig burger' – simply rip open a dried fig and stuff it with nuts!

EATING OUT

If you're asked out to dinner or have to travel over the next two weeks, don't panic!
You can stick to the programme and not go hungry – it's all about being prepared.
Here are some of our top tips for eating out while on a whole-food plant-based
diet. And see our tips for eating well when travelling, on page 193.

EATING AT A RESTAURANT

- Look at the restaurant's menu online and see if they have any suitable options.

- Call ahead and ask if they can cater to your needs. Chefs like to be challenged, and there is great interest at the moment in this way of eating.

- Go to ethnic restaurants if you can, as they will have the best selection of whole-food plant-based choices. Indian restaurants will always have a dahl (just be sure to check that it does not contain ghee – a clarified butter often used in Indian dishes). Mexican restaurants will usually have brown rice, beans and guacamole. A tasty stir-fry will always be available in Chinese restaurants, and Japanese restaurants will always have miso soup or sushi rolls made with avocado and cucumber – win!

- When we eat out we often order three or four side dishes, as these can be whole-food based.

- Eat before you go out so that you don't arrive starving. This means you can enjoy a few side dishes and not worry about feeling hungry.

EATING AT A FRIEND'S

- Tell your friends that your doctor has you on a diet. Once people think it is a medical choice, they are more likely to be understanding and supportive.

- Again, eating a light meal before you go out will help you to feel full if there is not much on offer.

- Bring a dish. Make one of the dishes from the meal plan and bring it with you. Bring extra too, as friends can be curious to try!

ALTERNATIVES TO DAIRY AND EGGS

Milk: These days there are a huge number of milk alternatives – rice, soya, oat, almond, coconut, hazelnut . . . we've even seen quinoa milk! If calcium is a concern, then buy one fortified with calcium. All plant-based milks are primarily made up of water and are less than 1% fat. Oat milk is our favourite. It's naturally creamy and quite neutral-tasting. Goes great on porridge or cereal. It also makes a great flat white.

Cheese: Dairy-free cheeses available in supermarkets and health food stores are made primarily of coconut oil and are high in fat. Nut cheeses are a great alternative and far healthier. However, just as with dairy cheeses, portion control is necessary! Stick to a portion no bigger than a small matchbox. Check out pages 139–41 for our dairy-free cheese recipes!

Butter: We don't recommend the current dairy-free butter alternatives, as they're highly processed and don't fit within a whole-food plant-based diet. Instead, we recommend using a thin spread of avocado – on a good day, Stephen's kids call avocado 'green butter', and love spreading it on rice cakes for a healthy snack!

Eggs: Here are some great alternatives to eggs that work just as well when baking.

Flax egg: Finely ground flax seeds act as a binder. The basic ratio is 1 tablespoon of ground flax seeds to 3 tablespoons of water, left to sit for 5 minutes.

Banana: A ripe banana can bring moisture and binding power to cakes and muffins. Depending on the recipe, use half a medium-size banana to replace 1 egg.

Chia seeds: Soaking chia seeds in water turns them to a gloopy consistency that can help to bind a mixture. A basic ratio is 3 tablespoons of water to 1 tablespoon of ground chia seeds, left to sit for 3–5 minutes.

LIFE AFTER THE TWO-WEEK HEALTH REBOOT

Just because you've completed two weeks – maybe you've lost some weight and you're more energetic – this does not mean that you have to pig out on all the junk food you haven't been eating!

Our health is based on what we eat most of the time, so sticking to a whole-food plant-based lifestyle as best you can will certainly help you to keep feeling and looking good. And the hope is that after two weeks, you'll have developed some habits that mean sustaining these positive changes becomes easier.

How you proceed after this course is totally up to you. We hope that we've shown you the benefits of a whole-food plant-based diet. However, this is not an all-or-nothing thing. Stick to what suits you and your lifestyle best. Find the point at which it is sustainable for you. You might follow the 80/20 rule – in other words, try to eat a whole-food diet 80% of the time. Or you might go plant-based Monday to Friday and allow yourself to eat more broadly at weekends. Or do a daily challenge: make one meal a day plant-based or make every meal except one plant-based. Another strategy is to be plant-based Monday to Sunday, except for dinner on a Friday night. Whatever way you do it, if you learn to tune in to your body – and the two-week challenge will help you do that – you will find yourself making the right choices for it.

We cannot stress enough that this is not about following a black and white ideal of being 'healthy' or 'unhealthy'. So even if the only long-term change you make is to have porridge for breakfast, or you swap white refined foods for brown wholegrain versions, or you find yourself snacking on hummus or fruit, we'll be delighted with that!

TWO-WEEK CHALLENGE Q&A

Q: I'm eager to cut down on my sugar intake, but it's hard. Can I use a sweetener?

A: We recommend reducing sugar intake without sweeteners as these can blunt your taste buds and your ability to detect natural sweetness in foods like fruits. Try to replace sweetness with dried fruits, as these are naturally higher in fibre and will slow down the release of the sugar – just make sure you brush your teeth after. If you're really struggling, wean yourself off slowly – so if you're having 2 teaspoons in a cup of tea, reduce it to 1½, then 1, then ½. It might take a few months, but it will be worth it.

Q: Is it OK to have diet drinks?

A: Synthetically sweetened beverages don't belong in a whole-food plant-based diet. Sweeteners do not promote good health and we recommend removing them completely from your diet.

Q: Are flax seeds and linseeds the same thing? Is it OK to buy them pre-ground?

A: Yes, they are – it's just different names for the same thing. Grinding them is our preference, but buying them pre-ground is fine. We advise keeping flax seeds in the fridge to prevent them from going rancid.

Q: Should I be careful of my salt intake?

A: We try to make our recipes as delicious as possible, and as chefs we're fond of a bit of salt to bring out flavour. A whole-food plant-based diet is naturally lower in salt, but if you have hypertension you need to be mindful of your salt intake. After years of offering this programme in classrooms, we've only ever seen blood pressure come down, not go up. That's Plant Power!

Q: Is this challenge suitable for coeliacs?

A: This course is not specially designed for people with coeliac disease, who have to avoid gluten. However, there are a lot of recipes that use tamari instead of soy sauce, or brown rice noodles instead of wholewheat noodles, for example, so a lot of them are naturally gluten free and can be enjoyed by people with coeliac disease. We recommend that you read all the recipes very closely and use substitutes where necessary.

Q: I have Type 2 diabetes. Is it OK to eat this many carbs?

A: Type 2 diabetes is one of the many chronic diseases where improvements can be made by making significant diet and lifestyle changes. We've replaced refined carbs with complex carbs on this course. Complex carbs have a very different glycaemic response, which shouldn't have any negative effect on people who have Type 2 diabetes. If in doubt, we recommend that you monitor your blood sugars and consult with your GP or nutritionist/dietician.

Q: What food sources are high in calcium and would be suitable for eating on the challenge?

A: Here are six great plant-based calcium sources:

- Tahini (426mg per 100g)
- Kale (150mg per 100g)

- Blackstrap molasses (205mg per 100g)
- Spinach (136mg per 100g)
- Fortified non-dairy milk (c. 120mg per 100ml)
- Tempeh (111mg per 100g)

Q: What foods are high in iron?

A: Beans, lentils, chickpeas and dark leafy veg (like kale, broccoli and cabbage) are super sources of iron, as are tofu and seeds. Cooking your meals in a cast-iron skillet will increase the amount of iron in your meal. Certain foods and drinks consumed with iron-rich foods will either increase or inhibit absorption. Tannins in tea and coffee inhibit iron absorption, whereas vitamin C-rich foods increase it.

Q: Is there a limit to the amount of nuts and seeds I should eat?

A: As with most things, there's a sweet spot between enjoying the food and avoiding excess consumption. Nuts and seeds are naturally high in fat and therefore in calories, but they are also rich in vitamins and minerals. We'd recommend 2-3 tablespoons a day.

Q: I struggle with snacking. Any tips?

A: We are serious snackers and use snacks to keep us energized between meals, so check out our snacks ideas on page 242. However, if you want to reduce your snacking but find yourself getting hungry between meals, try increasing the portion size of your main meals and use foods like quinoa, beans and legumes to get in a nice bit of nourishment and fibre, which keeps you feeling fuller for longer.

Q: What about coconut milk?

A: Using coconut milk sparingly in your meals is totally fine. It is high in fat, so you might want to swap your full-fat coconut milk for a lighter version.

Q: Is there a guideline to how much bread you could eat per day?

A: As long as it's made with 100% wholemeal flour, you can eat as much bread as you like! The high fibre content will fill you up and slow down the sugar release.

Q: Help! My gut doesn't know what's hit it – and I'm a bit windy!

A: If you're having trouble with all the excess fibre, don't worry, you're not alone. One of the most common bits of feedback we get on this challenge relates to increased bowel movements. There is no normal when it comes to bowel movements, but you might notice you've changed from once every two days, to twice in one day. As long as you have no pain, this is not something to worry about, and indeed, the more regularly you can eliminate waste, the better!

It's also not uncommon to experience increased bloating, flatulence and cramping when you've suddenly increased your fibre intake. Many people adjust after the first week, and it all calms down. However, if you feel worse as the course progresses, this could be an indication of Irritable Bowel Syndrome (IBS). Many of the foods that we advocate can cause problems for people diagnosed with IBS. These are beans, legumes, and certain veggies and fruits high in things called FODMAPs (types of fermentable carbohydrates that can increase bloating and cramping in susceptible individuals). If you suspect this is your problem, or if you're just not happy with how your gut is behaving, please consult your GP or dietician.

Q: I really struggle with finding time for exercise. Any advice?

A: Just do it . . . seriously!

We don't want to sound flippant, but that's our advice. All of us could use busyness as an excuse, because we're all pressed for time these days. Team up with a workout buddy and try to commit to something together – you are less likely to back out if someone else is depending on you. Or get a dog – it would be cruel not to walk the dog! Also, if you enjoy what you're doing you won't want to avoid it – so dance, run, swim, wall-climb, skate, skip . . . whatever makes you happy and gets those endorphins pumping along with your heart rate.

We both love this Zen proverb:

> *'You should sit in meditation for twenty minutes every day – unless you're too busy; then you should sit for an hour.'*

This applies to exercise. Even doing a little will improve blood flow and increase oxygen to your body, meaning you'll be more alert and ready for action!

'You should sit in meditation for twenty minutes every day — unless you're too busy; then you should sit for an hour.'

Zen proverb

REBOOT STORIES

BLAINE POWER (31)

Mam went plant-based first. I was having problems with my bowel and the surgeon said I couldn't digest meat any more. Mam was cooking Happy Pear food using the first two books. Then I gave up dairy.

BEFORE

AFTER

I was a wicked snorer and had sleep apnoea. My girlfriend said I used to stop breathing for 30 seconds at a time when I was asleep and she would have to give me a dig with her elbow just to see that I was still alive! The sleep apnoea went away as soon as I gave up dairy and meat.

I do a cook-up on a Sunday and have it for the week. I started in July 2016 and lost 5½ stone (35kg) in less than a year. My energy levels have gone way up and I need less sleep than before. I used to be always tired and would go to bed early. Now I go to bed around midnight and get up at 7 a.m. and have more energy than before. Plant-based food and cooking has changed my life.

THREE CHANGES THAT HELPED ME TO TURN MY LIFE AROUND:

- Eating organic produce and really noticing the difference in terms of taste.

- Feeling better in my own skin and much more confident.

- Getting massive support from my mam – she is vegan and really pushed me on (she had a dinner ready for me every evening and as soon as I felt the benefits I kept going myself).

ANGELA O'CALLAGHAN (51)

I had been four or five stone overweight since I had my first child in 2002. In the following years I had my second child and became a foster-mother to three children. I was so busy looking after everyone else that I forgot about myself and my health suffered as a result.

BEFORE   AFTER

In 2016 I attended a gastric surgeon about getting a gastric band fitted. On my way home from that visit, I decided to book my place on the Happy Heart course.

Since then I have lost two stone. I swim with my children several times a week, whereas before I wouldn't wear a swimsuit, for fear of embarrassment. Making healthy food choices comes naturally to me now and I feel motivated and focused.

THREE CHANGES THAT HELPED ME TO TURN MY LIFE AROUND:

- Planning and shopping for a meal plan per day based on recipes from the Happy Pear cookbooks and YouTube videos.

- Including some exercise throughout the week.

- Learning meditation, mindfulness and yoga.

MIA MCKAY (26)

I recently embarked on a plant-based diet and decided to sign up to the Happy Heart course to get inspiration. I didn't do it to lose weight, but I have lost a stone and have never felt healthier or more confident. Since eating the Happy Pear way, I sleep better, have more energy, my skin is clearer, and I feel stronger. I did not realize that healthy food would have such a positive impact on so many areas of my life.

THREE CHANGES THAT HELPED ME TO TURN MY LIFE AROUND:

- Listen to your body. If it feels good, you are doing the right thing.

- Be organized. Always having snacks to hand means you won't feel the urge to grab that piece of chocolate or a biscuit on the run.

- Don't worry about what other people have to say about what you are eating or not eating. It's your body and you are making changes for yourself and no one else.

AIDEEN QUIRKE (30)

I had been suffering from low energy levels for the past few years and was struggling to get out of bed for work or to socialize with friends. I am only thirty, so I knew something wasn't right.

After it was confirmed that I didn't have any serious health condition, my doctor recommended that I get involved in something that I had always loved but had lost interest in. For me, this was cooking and enjoying meals.

I signed up to the Happy Heart course and after the first week, I was hooked. I learned about food I had never heard of – for instance, I had thought that a celeriac was a person with some type of food allergy!

The benefits of the change in my diet were immediate. I lost weight, my skin became clearer and my nails stronger. Most important, eating this way restored my energy levels and boosted my motivation.

THREE CHANGES THAT HELPED ME TO TURN MY LIFE AROUND:

- Even a little effort goes a long way. A takeaway is not more convenient if a tasty dinner only takes 15 minutes to make!

- Every day you eat well, you feel well. Some days are more difficult than others, but you are just one healthy meal away from getting back on track.

- Be flexible. When you are meeting friends for lunch or have a family event, don't worry about what you can and can't eat, but plan ahead – David and Stephen have some great tips for this.

ALL ABOUT PLANT-BASED EATING!

Starting out on our Happy Heart course, where participants adopt a plant-based diet, on the first night there is often a sense of doom and *'Why did I sign up for this (stupid) course?'* Four weeks later, when we ask people how they got on, most participants say it was easier than they expected and that the benefits in terms of energy levels, weight loss and reduced cholesterol have far outweighed the effort.

The biggest misconception about a plant-based diet is that it means a life of deprivation, of eating nothing but kale! A whole-food plant-based diet is made up of fruits, vegetables, whole grains, beans, lentils, nuts, and seeds. It excludes anything that had a face or a mother – so that means all meat (including white meat such as chicken), all fish, all dairy products and eggs. It also excludes most refined and processed foods, such as refined flours, sugars and oils. We know it can sound restrictive, but our hope is that this book proves you can eat delicious satisfying plant-based meals.

Of course there's no such thing as perfect health, but in our experience of putting thousands of people on a plant-based diet, the more you stick to it, the better your health markers will be in terms of losing weight, having more energy, easily maintaining a healthy weight, lowering cholesterol and reducing high blood pressure, etc. We try to eat this way as much as possible, which is pretty much 99% of the time (the exception is cake!).

Good on you if you've dipped into the world of plant-based eating by doing the two-week health reboot! And good on you too if you're thinking of doing it. There is no pressure – it's there for you to try any time. Here's a quick explanation of why it works so brilliantly. Eating this way, you . . .

- **Naturally reduce saturated fat:** Saturated fat is found mainly in animal products and refined plant oils. Eating a whole-food plant-based diet eliminates most of these sources.

- **Naturally reduce dietary cholesterol:** Cholesterol is a type of fat found in every cell of our bodies. Too much cholesterol can stick to the walls of our arteries, leading to blockages, heart attacks and strokes. Other mammals also have cholesterol, and if we eat food from another mammal we're eating their dietary cholesterol too. On the other hand, whole foods such as fruits, veg, beans, whole grains, nuts and seeds contain no dietary cholesterol.

  When we've run the classroom Happy Heart course, and tested cholesterol levels at the start and at the end of the course, almost all participants saw a drop in their levels. The mechanism was most likely due to lowered intake (no dietary cholesterol), combined with increased output (excretion due to the extra fibre intake).

- **Increase your intake of fibre:** Fibre is found only in plant-based foods, such as vegetables, whole grains, fruits, nuts, beans and legumes. The more fibre in your diet, the better equipped your body is to eliminate waste, excrete cholesterol, maintain weight, and optimize immune function.

- **Increase your intake of antioxidants:** We all know antioxidants are good for us and help us to age more gracefully (that's why we lash into the blueberries first thing in the morning!). Brightly coloured foods are the primary source of antioxidants, so it's important to eat lots of bright-coloured fruit and veg, from purple (e.g. berries), to orange (e.g. carrots, sweet potatoes, squash), to red (e.g. beets, berries, tomatoes), to green (e.g. spinach, broccoli, kale, cabbage and also green tea). The more colours in your diet, the more antioxidants and the more protection you have against premature ageing.

---

1. https://www.ncbi.nlm.nih.gov/pubmed/21616193.

- **Reduce your intake of foods infused with antibiotics and artificial hormones:** Up to 80% of the antibiotics used are used in animal agriculture, to prevent infections spreading among animals kept in unhygienic and overcrowded conditions. Artificial hormones are also used to speed up their growth. These hormones can enter human circulation when the animal is eaten. This reduces the power of antibiotics to help us when we need them.

The rest of this section gives you a bit more detail on some of the key aspects of good nutrition that plant-based eating can help with.

WEIGHT

Wouldn't we all love to be able to eat our way to a slim body? Well, this is actually possible by eating the right type of foods. Unrefined, whole plant-based foods are naturally high in fibre (which fills you up – see the next section) and full of nutrition, while at the same time being low in calories, fat and salt. Because they're high in fibre you also avoid the spikes in blood sugar levels that you get with a diet of processed food.

The great thing about eating a whole-food plant-based diet is that you can stop calorie-counting, and you can be generous with your portions and satisfy yourself. Provided you are simply eating whole foods you can eat as much as you like and you will naturally lose excess weight, so it's a win-win situation! Studies have shown that, on average, vegetarians eat 363 fewer calories every day than omnivores[1] and that, on average, the only dietary pattern associated with the ideal body weight is a strictly plant-based one.

Although vegetarians are eating fewer calories per day, they have also been shown to get higher intakes of nearly every nutrient: more fibre, vitamin A, vitamin C, vitamin E, calcium, magnesium and potassium.

FIBRE

While vegans and vegetarians are familiar with the question, 'Where do you get your protein?' far fewer people ask us about fibre. Yet this is a huge area of deficiency in modern diets. A massive 97% of Americans are deficient in fibre,[2] and most of Western society is the same. While we should be aiming for in excess of 30g of fibre a day (some research recommends that we even get up to 60g per day), most of us are only getting a measly 14g!

Fibre is found only in plant foods, so foods such as meat, dairy, eggs and fish do not contain any fibre. Highly processed and refined foods also generally have very little or no fibre.

Most of us associate fibre with grade A digestion and yes, this is the case. It is essential to healthy digestion and a healthy bowel. But eating foods that are high in fibre can also help with weight loss, as they help us feel fuller for longer. Fibre fills our stomachs and stimulates stretch and density receptors that send signals to our brains that we are full. It also holds water in your stomach, so it's heavy enough to trick your stomach and then your brain into thinking you have eaten quite a lot.

Getting back to digestion, the bulk of our immune system is actually located in the digestive tract and depends on the health of our gut bacteria. As we have approximately 10 trillion human cells and approximately 100 trillion micro-bacteria, you could say that we are more bacteria hosts than we are human! The health and diversity of these gut bacteria directly affect the health of our immune system.

The micro-bacteria in our gut feed on fibre, which functions as a prebiotic. Prebiotics are like a fertilizer for all these micro-bacteria. The more of it you give them and the more varied it is, the more they thrive and the better for your immune system and overall health.

If you are not used to eating a high-fibre diet, you may find that you experience some excess wind or increased bowel movements. This is completely normal. Our digestive system is like a muscle, so just give it time to adjust and build strength and with time your body will get used to it.

---

2.   https://www.ars.usda.gov/ARSUserFiles/80400530/pdf/0102/usualintaketables2001-02.pdf.

FAT

Fat is essential to help our bodies to function optimally, provide us with a source of energy and help us absorb certain vitamins and minerals. It's better for you if the fats you eat are whole rather than refined. Whole fats are naturally occurring in foods that are naturally high in fat, such as avocados, nuts, seeds and olives. With these you are also getting fibre and lots of vitamins and minerals. The fats in these foods are predominantly healthier monounsaturated and polyunsaturated fats, and they include the essential fatty acids – omega-3 and omega-6 – which cannot be made by the body.

Refined fats are fats that have been processed in some way and that do not contain any nutrition other than fat. It is for this reason that we consider all oils to be a refined fat source – yes, even olive oil, so sorry to any Mediterranean diet fans out there! For example, olive oil is 100% fat, whereas an olive is typically approx. 15–30% fat content while also providing fibre, vitamins, and minerals. We do use oils in our cooking but we try to use them sparingly.

ESCAPING THE PLEASURE TRAP!

Both of us having young kids, we are very aware of just how addictive sweets and processed foods are. We have no doubt that our kids would nearly sell their granny for an ice cream! The pleasure trap explains why we love all the stuff that's bad for us. Things like doughnuts, croissants, chips, burgers, sweets, ice cream, all kinds of processed foods . . . in terms of how they combine salt, sugar and fat, and also their texture and appearance, they manage to hit what food scientists call 'the bliss point', which gives us a moment of pleasure. Dopamine, a neurotransmitter in our brain, takes note and urges us to do it again so we'll get the same rush of pleasure again.

This makes sense! Evolutionarily, high-calorie foods were more beneficial to us, as they meant we could go without food for longer when it was scarce. In hunter-gatherer times it was useful to have the brain urging us to eat calorie-dense foods: it meant we would survive and hopefully pass on our DNA. On the other hand, when food supplies were unreliable, depending on low-calorie food would risk your survival. In summary, it is completely natural to be addicted to refined fat, sugar and salt, i.e. the modern Western diet. It's our survival instinct at work.

The pleasure trap explains why it is difficult, and can seem less pleasurable in the short term, to switch to a healthier whole-food plant-based diet. Eating refined foods with high caloric density promotes hyperactive levels of dopamine release, convincing you that it is in your best interest to pursue that food. If you eat a lot of processed foods this becomes your normality, and whole-food plant-based diets seem bland and lacking in comparison. The taste receptors in your tongue tell you that you are moving in the wrong direction. This is what makes the pleasure trap so frustrating: when you do the right thing it feels wrong, and when you do the wrong thing it feels right!

Our recipes are packed full of flavour and texture, but if you've been eating a very heavily processed diet you may still find it an adjustment to move to more plant-based eating. However, if you persevere for several weeks your taste buds will re-sensitize, and you will regain your ability to get pleasure from real foods. (Anyone who has ever given up sugar in their tea will know exactly what we mean – you keep reducing until the point that if someone gave you a cup of sugary tea, you couldn't drink it!)

Key to escaping the pleasure trap is knowing that it exists. So when you adjust your diet to more whole foods, even if it doesn't seem as exciting at first, holding on to the knowledge that you are breaking free from a trap will help you stay focused. And the good news is that your body will get used to a new normal!

If you have been trying to do well and then succumb to a weekend of indulgence, you're back into the dietary pleasure trap and a healthy meal isn't going to taste as good to you. The solution: let yourself get hungry! On Monday morning don't eat for a while. Try to go all the way to Monday afternoon or evening. The sensitivity of your taste receptors will increase, your motivation for eating will rise, and once you have a healthy meal, you increase the likelihood of enjoying that meal. Getting hungry is a quick way to try to move through this trap – as our grannies used to say: hunger is great sauce!

A second technique is to use juice fasting for a day or two. If you drink a fresh vegetable juice you are taking all the fat and salt out of your diet. In doing so you are resting those receptors and increasing their sensitivity. This can be a very useful short-term manoeuvre to help you on your way out of the pleasure trap.

WHAT'S ON THE LABEL

Food labels can be confusing and statements such as 'low fat' and 'no sugar' can often be misleading. Here are some tips for reading labels and being a savvy shopper:

- First, try to eat more foods that do not have labels! Following a whole-food plant-based diet means eating mainly unrefined and unprocessed foods that do not need a label.

- Never believe what is written on the front of a product – it is there to sell the product. Anyone can write 'healthy'. Often 'low fat' means high sugar.

- Read the ingredient list and aim for foods that have a very short list of only recognizable ingredients. The ingredient list is in descending volume order – what is first on the ingredient list is most in the product and what is last is least in the product.

- There are many words for sugar. Pay attention to ingredients that end in 'ose' – this is usually a form of sugar. Often food products can have a number of different forms of sugar to avoid listing sugar as one of the main ingredients, e.g. a product might list corn syrup, inverted grape syrup and maltodextrin so that all three sweeteners end up in the middle of the ingredient list, whereas if they used one sweetener it would come at the top of the ingredient list.

- When it comes to buying bread, look for those described as 100% wholegrain or 100% wholemeal. For all grains it needs to say **WHOLE** on the packaging to ensure that it is actually whole (don't get distracted by 'organic', 'Fairtrade', etc.).

- Check the nutritional information panel. Ideally fibre will be at least 3g, to indicate that it's mostly whole-food based. Sugar content should be looked at in conjunction with fibre, e.g. a 100g dried fruit bar might have 'carbohydrates – of which sugars 47g' but a fibre content of 6g. That is high in fibre and indicates the sugar is coming from a whole-food source (the dried fruit). Compare that to, say, a Mars bar with 60g of sugar and 1.2g of fibre. Clearly the sugar is coming from a refined source.

FAQs ABOUT PLANT-BASED EATING

The questions here are based on the Q&A sessions we've done on social media, at our Happy Heart courses and at other events – plus stuff people ask us all the time! We are not medical doctors or dieticians, so our answers are based on our own experience over seventeen years.

Q: How much sleep do you get?

A: Having young kids, it's not easy to get a set amount every night. We try to get to sleep before 10 p.m. and then get up at what's deemed pretty early for most people – usually around 5 a.m. This allows us to make time for a daily swimrise (see page 286) and morning training before the day unfolds.

Q: How do you feel about alcohol?

A: Alcohol is the epitome of a refined food. We generally advise anyone who wants to improve their health to cut down or eliminate alcohol from their diet. But if a glass of Rioja makes the thought of a meat-free, veg-filled dinner more pleasing, then by all means go for it. Just keep it to a minimum and be mindful of the foods you're craving the next day – keep them whole-food and plant-based and you'll be grand!

Q: And what about caffeine?

A: As any coffee drinker knows, caffeine is great for sharpening your focus and helping you with tasks that might need your sustained concentration. We don't drink coffee daily, but occasionally, when we feel our tanks are running empty and we need a little kick-start, we will share an espresso. We recommend you limit your caffeine intake to either 1–2 cups of coffee per day or 2–3 cups of breakfast or green tea per day. Change all other coffees/teas to herbal tea or warm water. Use your favourite non-dairy milk as needed.

Q: What's your view on coconut oil?

A: From our experience, and in line with medical opinion, it's best to eat as little saturated fat as possible. Coconut oil has a very high saturated fat content – about 90% – so while it works great when applied directly to skin or hair (it makes both silky smooth – give it a try!), we use it sparingly in cooking. However, we don't believe in demonizing food, and coconut oil serves a purpose as a natural fat to make cakes and sweet treats deeeelicious!

Q: I eat a vegan diet; should I supplement vitamin B12?

A: From statistics that we've read, 4 out of 10 people are deficient in B12 and that's across the general population, not just vegans or vegetarians. Every time we've been tested over the last fifteen years, we've had healthy B12 levels. In saying that, after listening to the views of Dr Michael Gregor (nutritionfacts.org), who stresses the huge importance of B12 in a healthy lifestyle, we occasionally take supplements. But it's more as a precaution rather than because of any deficiency.

Q: Do carbs make people fat?

A: In our experience, whole grains – brown rice, brown pasta, 100% wholegrain/wholemeal bread – will do the opposite of making you fat. These carbs are low in fat, sugar and calories and keep things moving along nicely in your gut.

Q: Is bread healthy?

A: It depends on what's in it. A lot of the bread available is made from refined white flour and has other additives to make it last longer. This is not good for you. Sourdough bread is all the rage now, and it is great in many ways, but in most cases it is still made with refined white flour. We recommend adding 100% wholegrain/wholemeal bread to your diet. Wholemeal pittas are a great option too – they are readily available in most supermarkets and are great toasted for lunch. Dave toasts these and cuts them into soldiers to put into his kids' lunchboxes along with hummus. Try our bread recipes on pages 36, 39 and 162.

Q: I'm dairy-free and plant-based and concerned about my calcium intake and whether I'm getting enough to ensure my bones stay healthy and strong.

A: We are all conditioned to believe that calcium comes from milk and dairy products. However, the real source of calcium is in the soil. Like iron, magnesium and copper, calcium is a mineral that is absorbed into the roots of plants as they grow. Typically animals get their calcium by consuming calcium-rich plants. A diet full of fresh fruit, veg and whole foods has more than enough calcium to meet our needs and keep bones healthy and strong. The highest sources of easily absorbable calcium can be found in dark green leafy vegetables like rocket, broccoli, kale, watercress (to maximize absorption, add a bit of vitamin C, e.g. lemon juice). Seeds are also an excellent source, particularly sesame seeds.

To maintain bone health, engaging in some form of moderate weight-bearing activity is as important as consuming adequate calcium. It is only when they are stressed and moved that the osteoblasts in our bones actually absorb the calcium.

Q: I'm tired all the time – how do I get more energy?

A: This whole book is about eating more whole plant foods, as they will give you a more sustained supply of energy. As a rule, processed foods will give you an energy peak, followed by a drop that will sap you of energy.

We are mammals and need to move, so make sure to have some form of movement/exercise as part of your day – it could be as simple as going for a walk.

After oxygen, water is our next most important fuel source – see the next question. Keep an eye on your urine and if it is yellow, drink more water.

Finally, maybe you are spending too much time doing things that are of no interest to you! Most people have no problem getting up early to get a flight to go on their holidays, but struggle to get up early to do something they don't like. Even if you're stuck in a job you don't like and can't get out of, see if there is some aspect of it you can engage with positively and focus on that.

Q: My iron levels are low and I'm low in energy – how can my diet help this?

A: Fatigue could be related to any number of things, e.g. lack of sleep, lack of exercise, mental health conditions or other nutrient deficiencies. But if you've seen a doctor and they've highlighted an iron deficiency, here's how you can bump up your intake:

- It's really important to incorporate vitamin C into your diet. Just 50mg of vitamin C (the amount in half a large orange) will enhance iron absorption by 3-6 times. Reach for foods like peppers, tomatoes, broccoli, cauliflower, oranges, kiwi and Brussels sprouts, which turn your body into a total iron-sponge!

- Greens such as broccoli, chard, spinach and pak choi are packed with iron, so stock up on these foods as well as fermented foods like sauerkraut and kimchi.

- Beans and quinoa also contain high amounts of iron. It's really good to pair these with orange/yellow vegetables such as pumpkin, yellow peppers, sweet potatoes and carrots (as well as garlic and onion) because these contain beta-carotene, which increases the absorption of iron from grains. When it comes to grains, the iron is concentrated in the outer layers – the germ and bran – which are removed in refining, so that's another reason to avoid white carbs.

Q: How much water should I drink a day?

A: We don't follow the mantra of 2 litres a day because this depends on the weather and what you eat. When you're eating whole plant foods it's mostly water anyway, and we don't want to spend our time running to the toilet. Just keep an eye on your urine and check that it's light in colour.

Q: How do I beat the afternoon slump?

A: *Move!* This might involve doing a few press-ups or star jumps, even a brisk walk for 5 minutes. In our experience, when we feel a little dopey or stagnant, movement is the quickest way of getting the oxygen into our body to energize our brains. See more about the benefits of exercise on page 279.

Q: My kids hate vegetables – how can I get more veg into their diet?

A: Cut them up super-small and hide them in dishes! Blending them in soups works great. If your kids will eat veggie burgers or falafel nuggets, these are good and easy. Our kids eat these. Smoothies and juices are a really good way – try to ensure they are more veg- than fruit-based. In terms of making your own juices for kids, it's best to start them drinking sweeter juices and gradually incorporate more veg until the juice is mostly made of veg. This is what we did with our kids and now their norm for juice is beetroot, carrot, celery, a little apple and some lime.

Trying to make veg more fun also can work well. We put veg crudités in our kids' lunchboxes each day and they eat them most of the time. Our kids like small, easy-to-hold pieces of cucumber, carrot and pepper.

Another option is to try to make it more fun. Check out Google or Pinterest for images of creative people making snails out of a stick of celery, a slice of cucumber and some almond butter, or Hallowe'en ghosts out of bananas and raisins!

Q: My son is 16, big into sports and building muscle. He takes a load of whey protein shakes and eats chicken breasts with every meal. Can he build muscle on a plant-based diet?

A: Parents of teenage boys often ask us this question. There is a misconception that you need to eat meat to get 'big', and people still believe that meat = muscle. What a teenager in this situation actually needs is plenty of calories from a wide variety of whole plant foods. Protein needs are easily met on a whole-food plant-based diet. All whole plant foods contain protein and will provide the recommended intake, which is approximately 10% of total caloric intake. This level of protein is what's needed for muscle repair and growth. The other important thing is to eat enough healthy carbs to fuel the body through demanding workouts.

The boys who are eating pounds of chicken and guzzling protein shakes probably think that if you're plant-based you're going to be weak and skinny and not at the races at all. However, there has been a massive rise in the number of top athletes eating plant-based diets over the last few years. Here are just some:

Rich Roll – cited by *Men's Health* magazine in 2012 as one of the 25 fittest men on the planet. He is an ultra-endurance athlete who completed five Ironman distance triathlons on five different Hawaiian islands in under a week. He says that the holy grail of sport is recovery and rapidly overcoming inflammation so you can train more. A whole-food plant-based diet causes the least possible amount of inflammation, meaning the body recovers much quicker.

Lionel Messi, one of the best footballers in the world, today eats a mostly vegan diet.

Two all-time tennis greats – Venus Williams and Novak Djokovic – eat a mainly vegan diet (Djokovic includes a little fish occasionally).

Kendrick Farris, the only man in the US weight-lifting team for the 2016 Olympics in Rio, sticks to a plant-based diet.

Even in combat sports like MMA – not a sport in which you would expect to find many plant-based athletes – more of them are popping up and defying the stereotype. In 2016 Nate Diaz, who eats a plant-based diet, defeated the world-famous UFC world title holder Conor McGregor.

Mac Dansig is also another plant-powered UFC champion.

British heavyweight boxing champion David Haye eats a plant-based diet and argues that as long as you eat enough, you'll have all the strength you need.

Plant-based athletes seem to thrive in endurance running and triathlons. Scott Jurek is a world-class endurance running legend and author of one of our favourite books (*Eat & Run*).

Dave Scott holds the record for the most Ironman World Championship victories ever, and is also plant-powered.

World champion surfer Tia Blanco is also vegan.

This is just a small sample of the world-class sportsmen and women thriving on plant-based diets. Tell your teenager to check them out if they're thinking the only way to be strong and healthy for their sports is loading up on meat and protein shakes!

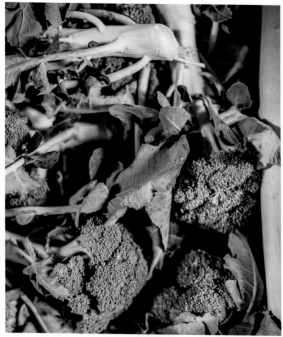

OUR FUNDAMENTALS OF HAPPINESS

In our experience happiness is all about food, movement and managing your head! And all these things are interrelated – if you can get into a good space with all three, you will give yourself the best chance of living a happier life and also be in a position to deal with the inevitable stresses and occasional upsets that life throws your way.

FOOD

The most important predictor of happiness in life is our health, and our health is hugely influenced by what we eat. It goes without saying that for us, food is very central to feeling good. This whole book is about food and about embracing the benefits that eating whole plant foods brings, so we won't talk about that again here other than to say it's not just about physical well-being. Having shifted our diets back in 2001, we got so much more out of it than just becoming healthier. It seemed to be a gateway to connecting with ourselves. We got away from feeling we had to aspire to what society said twenty-something men should (big jobs, flash cars, loads of money), and instead it helped us to see what was really important in life: striving for something worthwhile that was good for the planet, being positive, connecting with our community.

MOVEMENT
(MORE COMMONLY KNOWN AS EXERCISE!)

We are all mammals – highly sophisticated mammals with names, jobs, money and social structures. But underneath we are still mammals, and one thing all mammals have in common is the need to move. Dog owners know what we're talking about! What happens if you forget to walk your dog for a day? It gets pretty wired and wound up. And if you don't bring it out on day 2 or for a couple more days it will most likely have started to get lethargic and depressed-looking. Humans are very much like dogs in this respect – we need to move. Look at little kids: they move and also smile and laugh so much more than us adults.

Our primary fuel source is not food, or even water – it's oxygen. Without food you could probably last a month or so. Without water you could maybe last a week. But without oxygen you will die in a matter of minutes. Oxygen gives you energy, and how you get more oxygen into your body is by moving it. Once you move, your lungs take in more oxygen, your heart pumps the blood and oxygen around your body and WHAM, you feel more alert, awake and alive. So to beat the mid-afternoon slump, don't turn to coffee and a sweet snack – instead, move!

Think of movement/exercise as a magic pill that makes you feel good, helps you to lose weight and helps just about every system in your body to function better. It's a medicine in its own right, and as much for mental as physical health.

Throughout our lives we have always needed to move a lot – we are a bit like dogs in that respect! Movement has always been something that we needed to do – to feel good, to de-stress, to give us lots of energy. Many times since having kids we have made a New Year resolution to exercise more. But it wasn't really until 2016, when our friend Raj quit the gym and convinced us to train first thing in the morning before swimming in the sea, that we found a routine that we could stick to. It's become a habit now, and most days we have had a swim and trained before 7 a.m. and it's the cornerstone of our day.

To be technical about it, there are three aspects of exercise that we should all, ideally, be doing:

Cardiovascular – This is the most common form of exercise that people engage in and is all about getting your lungs pumping oxygen around your body. Walking, swimming, cycling are all good forms of cardio.

Flexibility – This is not about being able to bend your leg around your head or doing the splits (although we aspire to doing both!). This is about being able to bend over to pick something up and not pop your back. It gets more important as we age and our joints tend to stiffen up.

Strength – The aim here is not to bench-press 150kg or get big biceps. It's about being able to lift your suitcase when you go on holidays. Strength work is very important for maintaining strong healthy bones and absorbing calcium as we age. Any form of weight-bearing activity is great for this. Even simple things like walking and swimming do the job – in those cases, the weight you are bearing is your own body.

To benefit from exercise you don't have to have a six-pack or be toned all over. In fact, to benefit from exercise a lot less is required than most people think. If you are out of the habit of exercising, here are some suggestions for getting started again.

- You don't need to join a gym or a triathlon club or get new gym gear. It's as simple as walking for 30 minutes a day, and it doesn't even have to be in one go, it can be three short walks of 10 minutes. Studies have shown that you get most of the benefit of exercise by simply walking for 30 minutes a day.

- A dog can make a great walking coach, as it needs a walk every day, and you can't make excuses in the face of those puppy eyes!

- In terms of exertion, it is not a case of no pain, no gain. If you are walking, ensure that you can still hold a conversation but could not sing a song! That's the right level of breathing to get the best out of it.

- Get support from a friend. Exercising with others means you hold each other accountable. We find this so true with our morning training – if a couple of us are away we find it much harder to train alone. Training with others is more fun, and we often push ourselves to do things we could never have done alone.

- It doesn't have to be walking. Find some sort of activity that you enjoy and spend the time doing that. It could be gardening, swimming, jumping on a pogo stick, dancing . . . you get the idea.

- The best time to exercise will be different for everyone. Just make sure that you schedule it for a time when you know you can do it. For some it may be first thing in the morning, as you know nothing will get in your way. For others it may be in the evening, after the day's work is done, and you can use it to help you unwind and let go of the day. Or a brisk walk at lunchtime may be your best opportunity to move and it also refreshes you for the afternoon.

Once you get started you will soon begin to really feel the benefits, and quite quickly you won't want to miss it, as it is so important to making you feel good.

'It is about having a couple of things that you do for yourself, that
make you feel more yourself and help you recharge your batteries.'

MANAGING YOUR HEAD

Modern life can be so overwhelming. There's email and texts and WhatsApps and getting eight hours' sleep and staying fit and eating healthy and being nice and not upsetting the apple cart and keeping up at work and finding the perfect relationship . . . it's full on!

With all the demands on our time and attention, you can understand why mindfulness activities are becoming more relevant and popular than ever. They are a way to connect us back to ourselves and back to the present moment and to calm our busy minds. For many, this interest in mindfulness and meditation seems very 'new age' and fluffy – as our mom would say, 'Self-indulgent navel-gazing!' (*we love your honesty, Mom!*) – but we all want to be at our best and it's about figuring out what works for you. For some it might be meditation. For others it might be having a pint with friends in the pub or spending time with the kids/grandkids or a swim in the sea. Dave loves to have a good soak in a bath a couple of times a week. It is about having a couple of things that you do for yourself, that make you feel more yourself and help you recharge your batteries. Because you can't give to others if you are running on empty.

Sleep is a big part of managing your head. As we know, experts say we should get about eight hours' sleep a night. As those of you who follow us on social media know, we generally get up in time to appreciate the sunrise. We wake up at an hour that seems ungodly to most people, particularly in June, when we have to be up by 4.30 a.m. to get to the beach in time (read about our swimrises on page 286!). So we get asked all the time, 'How much sleep do you get?' We want to stress that just like everyone else we need our sleep too. We balance our early starts with early bedtimes (or as early as our young kids will allow). Rising at 4.30 a.m. and going full tilt all day means that by 9 o'clock we are typically fit for the bin and ready for bed.

Everyone's body clock is different and we all have different priorities and lifestyles. We don't drink alcohol or smoke, and having young families means that our socializing is done during the day. This is what works for us – for others it might be getting up late and staying up late. So whether you are an owl or a lark, do what works for you. Just don't try to burn the candle at both ends!

The other element of keeping your head well is connecting properly with other people. The difference between the words 'illness' and 'wellness' is small – one starts with 'I' and the other with 'we'. It's a nice way of saying that we are social creatures that do better together. Yet, even though we are more connected than ever through social media, mobile phones and the internet, loneliness seems to be a real epidemic. The power and importance of togetherness – through family, friends and community – cannot be underestimated. Together we can accomplish so much more.

VITAMIN SEA

Our interest in sunrises commenced in 2010 when Dave's elder daughter, Elsie, was a baby. Dave used to be out on the empty streets of Greystones in the early hours trying to walk her back to sleep. One summer morning he took a photo of the sunrise and shared it on Facebook. People went mad for that gorgeous view and so began our love of sharing sunrises!

Since summer 2016 we have been swimming at sunrise too, which kicked off our daily swimrise tradition. A lovely community of like-minded, brave souls has developed and we meet at the beach every morning for our 'morning wash', followed by a huddle around a warm cup of tea and good chats.

The swimrise is a magic way to start the day and very symbolic too. As soon as our heads hit the water we feel so much more alive and connected to ourselves and nature. The cold sea is so bracing that our worries and stresses seem to disappear. And if you can get up and have a swim in the cold sea first thing in the morning, then after that everything seems easier! Even on the coldest day of the year, when there was frost on the beach, there were fifteen of us lined up like penguins for our daily dip. It seems mad, but the camaraderie, the endorphins and the togetherness make it so worthwhile. Our swimrise intersects with so many aspects of life that we really value:

Connection to nature. Our morning ritual connects us with nature, the seasons and the outdoors. The sky, the shore and tides are different every single morning and we are more aware of and in tune with the environment around us.

A sense of freedom. In some magical way, swimming in the cold sea makes us feel freer. We always get out of the water in a better mood than we get in. Ruth Fitzmaurice, who swims with us in Greystones, describes it like this in her wonderful book, *I Found My Tribe*: 'I don't always like the person getting in the water, but I always love the person getting out.' That sums it up perfectly!

Community. The fabulous group of friends that we share this daily life-affirming activity with just seems to get bigger every day, as more people join from far and wide. It's an eclectic bunch of people from all walks of life and of all ages that come together to get their dose of Vitamin Sea!

INDEX

Recipe pages are in bold.

THANK YOU ☺

Our names are on the front of this book but really we have relied on the massive and continued help and support of so many people to get it over the line.

First, thanks to our families for putting up with the extra workload while we were writing and shooting. To Justyna, May, Theo and Ned; to Janet, Elsie and Issy; to Mum and Dad, Ismay and Donal, for always being there when we need support; to Darragh for being the engine in the HP and as much a part of this story as we are; to Mark for your help and support from a distance and for your clear brotherly perspective; to Yeşim for putting our recipes into a coherent form for sending off to Penguin, and for your Mom's wonderful Turkish leek recipe which we first ate at your and Darragh's wedding in Turkey and have enjoyed many times since!

Thanks to the fantastic Sarah Fraser in Penguin's art department for putting so much into this project, it really is such a pleasure working with you and it's great to see our friendship grow over three books now! From styling shots to the final design your great eye for beauty and detail has been invaluable in creating this lovely book. Thanks also to the other designer who contributed to this book: Gail Jones. Thanks for David Ettridge for all the behind-the-scenes logistics in the art department. And a massive shout-out to John Hamilton for overseeing and driving on this project and for keeping a watchful eye on it – you are brill and a total dude!

Thanks to Alistair Richardson for doing such an amazing job photographing this book (and our previous two). We always look forward to book shoots with you and Sarah, such a lovely team has formed. Your photos get better and better and we greatly value what you do. You have become a lovely friend over the three books now. Also to Seánie Cahill for shooting supplementary photography throughout the book – thanks for working so closely with us and for your friendship. You are a great man and a dear friend and thanks for all your input into this book food-wise too!

Thanks to Orla Neligan for your fantastic work styling all the recipe photos – your eye for detail is second to none. And a big shout-out to Article Dublin, The Props Library, Folkster, Meadows & Byrne, M&S, Avoca and Dunnes Stores who provided all the necessary pots, pans and props needed to help make the food and the final photos look amazing. Thanks also to Bella O'Keeffe for all the good energy you brought during the shoot and for your hard work.

Thanks to Geraldine Carton for your fab help, particularly with the two-week reboot and the fundamentals of happiness chapters. You are always such a pleasure to work with, a brilliant writer and a lovely friend.

Thanks to Susan McKeever for editing the recipes so brilliantly. And thanks to Annie Lee for all your top-class copy-editing. You are a pleasure to work with as always and have an amazing eye for detail.

Thanks to our agents, Faith O'Grady and Eavan Kenny, you guys are brill and a pleasure to work with.

Thanks to our wonderful editor, Patricia Deevy, for putting your heart and soul into this project too. You are amazing and we love you dearly and thanks for all your support and guidance and your incredible work ethic, our respect for you has only grown over three books now! Thanks to Michael McLoughlin, Patricia McVeigh, Cliona Lewis, Carrie Anderson, Brian Walker and all the team in Penguin Ireland. In London, thanks to Joanna Prior for your support and always being so lovely to deal with. Also at 80 Strand, thanks to Keith Taylor (happy retirement, Keith!), Emma Brown, Annie Underwood, Amelia Fairney, Poppy North, Rose Poole, Cat Mitchell, Sam Fanaken and Catherine Wood – all of whom have been vital in helping us in different ways.

Thanks to our dear friend Tamsin English for getting the whole process started three books ago. This third book would not have happened without you kicking it all off! We love you dearly!

Next, thanks to the fantastic team that makes the Happy Pear what it is. Without you there would be no Happy Pear. Thanks to Donal, Darragh and Paul Murphy for directing the show. Paul, as our new financial director, you have been wonderful to work with and spend time with – your tastings and feedback were very much appreciated! Thanks to Sarah Dunne who keeps us in check and organizes our lives in so many ways, you're brilliant and we love you and are so grateful.

Thanks to Jonny O'Donohue for being the 'Lord Mayor' of Pearville and always going the extra mile. Thanks to Gerard and Sean in NPD, Paula in Quality, to Lindy for your brilliant designs and your contagious zest for life. On our People Ops team, thanks to Conor Kirwan, Anne-Marie Griffin for doing such an amazing job this year along with Natalie. In IT, thanks to Alan Keighery and Michelle. In Finance, thanks to Jane, Val and Lorraine for being so meticulous and so lovely to have around. In Sales and Marketing, thanks to Patrick and Avril, Chris Peare, Fiona McBennett, and Roisin. On the road, thanks to Jer, Gerry, Catherine, Cousin Paul, Joan and Brian. In the Warehouse, thanks to Wayne, Maurice, Sandis, Andrezej, Szymon, Peter, John, Jordan, Kris Tate and Dennis. On the blending team, thanks to Dee, Anne Crotty, Alan, Darren, Apple, Lillian, Stephen and Helen for being such amazing people and being so consistent and hard-working. In Fermenting, thanks a mil to Magda. In Church Road, thanks to Enya, Katie, Marty, Kate, Adam, Giuliano, He Cha, Jamie, Shane, Serene, Daniel, William and Fiona. In our newest cafe and shop in Clondalkin, thanks to Mark Matanes, Lauren, Nikki, Nadya, Peter, Noeleen and Sadhbh and all our wonderful team there – you are doing an amazing job, thank you! On our farm, thanks to Stephen, Niamh, Tomek, Dylan and Lene. In our cafe in Shoreline, thanks to Elaine, Anto, Julie and Ciara.

Thanks to Hannah Mangan for testing lots of the desserts and for being the lovely face of the front desk of Pearville, you're a great part of the team. A special thanks to Kevin Mulvaney for trialling loads of the recipes and being a part of this book - it was brilliant to have you help so much on the shoot days and to have someone that understood how we work from helping with our previous book, thank you.

Thanks to our cousin, Naomi Smith, for putting your heart and soul into the HP (and to little Paddy Lyons). To Juan, our head chef, for your commitment, your wonderful manner and your great work and food. Thanks to Jennifer, our head baker, for all your hard work and being so accommodating with all our requests! Thanks for trialling and looking over many of the cake recipes. Also, thanks to Leah and the rest of the fab bakers - Netty, Laura, and to Gong Ping, He Qiang, Toni, Giuliano, Will, Santan, Michael and Mickey for your incredible hard work.

Thanks to Paul Grimes and Shane Murphy, the coffee maestros - you are both legends! Thanks to Namey D, Yuri, Santo Christiano and Dougie. Thanks to Rajdeep Singh, for all your incredible cheer, constant support and wonderful friendship - you're one in a million!

Siobhán Hanley, our woman-of-all-trades and fairy godmother, thanks for being so supportive, caring and amazing over the years.

Thanks to all our elders - Alan Smith, Ashley Glover, Rod Large, Aidan O'Byrne and Amory Schwartz, you guys are a great sounding-board and wise dudes whose help we are very grateful for! Thanks to all our lovely suppliers - thanks for your great produce and service, you are all central to what we do.

Thanks to our brilliant Swimrise and training family - you guys are amazing and we love you dearly! Julie, Thomas, Niall, Caroline, Ciara, Ed, Hugo, Treasa, Haelee, Enya, Sarah, Ciara, Katie and Joe, Olivia, Conor, Orla, Innes, Michelle, Ruth.

Finally, thanks to the people of our hometown of Greystones and our extended community. Thank you for your support - without it there would be no Happy Pear!

Lastly and so importantly, thanks to all our customers and supporters - we're so grateful.

Yours

Dave & Steve xx

HOW TO DO A HANDSTAND!

We got into doing handstands years ago and love to spend time upside down each day – it gives us a different perspective and pumps oxygen around our bodies, making us feel good and waking us up when we feel tired. Handstands may not be for everyone (and we had to twist our editor's arm to put this in the book) – consider this a bonus track for the truly hard-core fans!

Getting started is usually the hardest part. The handstand does not require great strength, and the strength needed is easier to build than most people think, so long as you practise frequently. The big challenge is overcoming your fear of being upside down or falling over. With practice, you'll overcome that.

Practising handstands just once a week is not enough, particularly if you want to master it in a month or two. Even three times a week isn't ideal. In our experience, doing it correctly for five minutes a day over one to two months is a realistic time frame and will produce the best results. We give you the basics below. Once you can do each of these steps the world is your oyster in terms of handstands and you will be ready to start freestyling away from the security of the wall you use in practice! This is a super-basic guide, so watch a few beginners' videos on YouTube to better understand it . . . and stay safe!

1. **60-second wall plank:** Go into a plank pose – feet towards the wall. Move your hands towards the wall and toes up the wall slightly. Hold. Try to keep your body straight, and parallel to the ground. Practise this until you can hold it for 60 seconds. Practise getting your hands closer to the wall and your toes further up it.

2. **60-second wall handstand:** Walk your legs up the wall until your face and belly button are facing it. Remember to keep your back straight and your head down. Work at being able to hold this position for 60 seconds. As you get more confident, start bringing your hands closer to the wall so that eventually they are just 30cm from the base of the wall and you are practically fully upside down. You're doing a handstand!

3. **Bailing out of a handstand:** This is the most important part of learning to do a handstand. Push one of your feet against the wall hard enough that your weight shifts away from the wall. Gravity will take its course and you will be able to come down safely.

4. **Freestanding handstand:** There are two methods here. First, follow steps 1 and 2 but then tap your feet away from the wall so you're no longer using it for support. Once you're confident doing it this way, face the wall and kick up into a handstand (so your back is facing the wall) – it will take practice to be able to kick into a handstand. Lean the backs of your feet against the wall and slowly learn to hold one foot off the wall and then both feet – hold for one second at a time until you can gently kick off the wall and hold it for 15 seconds. Bail out safely. Practise until you no longer need to lean your feet on the wall at all. Once you've mastered that, you can do your handstands anywhere!

PENGUIN IRELAND

UK | USA | Canada | Ireland | Australia
India | New Zealand | South Africa

Penguin Ireland is part of the Penguin Random House group of companies
whose addresses can be found at global.penguinrandomhouse.com.

First published 2018
001

Colour reproduction by Altaimage Ltd
Printed in China

A CIP catalogue record for this book is available from the British Library

ISBN: 978-1-844-88425-4

www.greenpenguin.co.uk